PENGUIN BOOKS

ALL POINTS NORTH

Simon Armitage was born in West Yorkshire in 1963. In 1992 he won one of the first Forward Prizes for poetry, and a year later was the *Sunday Times* Young Writer of the Year. His *Selected Poems* appeared in 2001, and in 2007 he published a highly praised translation of *Sir Gawain and the Green Knight*. He received an Ivor Novello Award for his song lyrics in the BAFTA-winning film *Feltham Sings*. First published in Penguin in 1999, *All Points North* is now reissued with Armitage's new book, *Gig*. He works as a freelance writer, broadcaster and playwright, and has written extensively for radio and television.

Simon Armitage lives near Huddersfield with his wife and daughter.

Simon Armitage

ALL POINTS NORTH

PENGUIN BOOKS

PENGUIN BOOKS

Published by the Penguin Group
Penguin Books Ltd, 80 Strand, London WC2R ORL, England
Penguin Group (USA) Inc., 375 Hudson Street, New York, New York 10014, USA
Penguin Group (Canada), 90 Eglinton Avenue East, Suite 700, Toronto, Ontario, Canada M4P 2Y3
(a division of Pearson Penguin Canada Inc.)
Penguin Ireland, 25 St Stephen's Green, Dublin 2, Ireland (a division of Penguin Books Ltd)
Penguin Group (Australia), 250 Camberwell Road, Camberwell, Victoria 3124, Australia
(a division of Pearson Australia Group Pty Ltd)
Penguin Books India Pvt Ltd, 11 Community Centre, Panchsheel Park, New Delhi – 110 017, India
Penguin Group (NZ), 67 Apollo Drive, Rosedale, North Shore 0632, New Zealand
(a division of Pearson New Zealand Ltd)
Penguin Books (South Africa) (Pty) Ltd, 24 Sturdee Avenue,
Rosebank, Johannesburg 2196, South Africa

Penguin Books Ltd, Registered Offices: 80 Strand, London WC2R ORL, England

www.penguin.com

First published by Viking 1998
Published in Penguin Books 1999
This edition published 2009

012

Copyright © Simon Armitage, 1998
All rights reserved

The moral right of the author has been asserted

Acknowledgements are due to Kim Flintcroft for his contribution to *Jerusalem*,
and also to Alison Carter of Holmes Associates, London

Printed in England by Clays Ltd, St Ives plc

ISBN: 978-0-141-04046-2

www.greenpenguin.co.uk

Penguin Books is committed to a sustainable
future for our business, our readers and our planet.
This book is made from Forest Stewardship
Council™ certified paper.

Contents

Contents

I was demoralized when I left Bradford for Florida . . . – Frederick Delius

The use of the pronoun 'one' to mean 'any person', 'I', or 'me' is often regarded as an affectation . . . *the less formal 'you' can usually replace it successfully and is safer when one is launching into a long statement.* – Concise Oxford Dictionary

I rode over the mountains to Huddersfield and a wilder people I never saw in all England. The men, women and children filled the streets as we rode along and appeared just ready to devour us. They were, however, tolerably quiet while I preached; only a few pieces of dirt were thrown. – John Wesley's Journal, June 1757

Where You're At

True story. Last winter, three men from a village in West Yorkshire went fishing off the coast near Scarborough, and hauled in an unexploded mine from the Second World War. A crowd gathered to look at the bomb, and a reporter from local television turned up to interview the men on the beach. When the reporter asked one of them if they'd been frightened, he said, 'No, we're alright, us.'

*

I live on the border, between two states. On the one hand, I am who I am, and I know who that person is. It's me, and I can prove it. I've got family and friends who'll vouch for me. I've got a birth certificate to show where I'm from, a passport that says where I've been, and neighbours who know where I live. I've lived here all my life, just about, and I know this place like the back of my hand. I know what I'm doing and I know what it's doing to me. And I know about belonging, and which of the people are my lot – us. We're a mixed bunch, although it's all relative, and one of us is no more mixed and no less relative than the rest. Me. On the other hand, sometimes it's somebody else. Those mixed-up days when it's easier to spot yourself in a crowd than recognize yourself in a mirror. On those occasions, it isn't me doing the rounds, getting about, going here, there and everywhere, but it isn't some stranger either. It's the other person, the second one. It's you.

You live on the border. It's a cultural fault-line, this side of it being the Colne Valley, West Yorkshire, the last set of villages strung out along the trans-Pennine A62. Over the hill on the other side is Saddleworth, Lancashire. Saddleworth used to be in Yorkshire but the Boundary Commission recognized the watershed for what it was. One day a sign appeared at the brow of the hill saying *Oldham Metropolitan Borough* in luminous green letters. The day after that, the sign was obliterated with a shotgun wound, and a hand-painted board with the word *Saddleworth* was planted in front of it, finished off with a huge white rose. The council took down the offending object but a couple of days later it was back, this time in metal, and the official sign torn up from the soil and left mangled on the hard shoulder. This went on for months until the council gave up or couldn't be bothered. Today, both signs stand next to each other, making whatever lies beyond a kind of no man's land. All we know is that this side is Yorkshire, always was, and on the other side the buses are a different colour. People setting off into Saddleworth for the day talk about 'going over the top', as if they shouldn't necessarily be expected back.

Bulletins arrive in various forms, telling you what you're like, who you are. In the morning it's the *Yorkshire Post*, in the evening it's the *Huddersfield Examiner*. At teatime, it's *Look North* with Mike MacCarthy and the beautiful Sophie Rayworth, or on 'the other side' it's *Calendar*, once the hot-seat of Richard Whiteley, the I Claudius of broadcasting. Most of the stories reported involve animals or murder, or ideally both, and occasionally make the national press. A couple of weeks ago, the *Six O'Clock News* reported that pipistrelle bats from Yorkshire have a different dialect from the same bats just over the border in Lancashire. Under the heading 'Batting for Yorkshire', a scientist explained that the bats not only have a separate vocabulary, but also 'talk' at different frequencies, making it impossible for the two groups to communicate and mix. The bottom line is that Yorkshire bats have deeper voices, and are less chatty. The scientist seemed to feel that this was some extraordinary discovery, but to anyone living around here, it made perfect sense. The first village 'over the top' might only be five miles away, but in terms of dialect and language it might as well be in Cornwall. 'Look', in their part of the world, rhymes with 'fluke' or 'spook'. So does 'book'. So does 'cook'. 'Look in the book to see how to cook' becomes a very strange business. If the War of the Roses ever kicks off again, this will be the front line, and anyone crossing the divide will have to keep their traps tightly shut.

Of course, accents are what other people have. Further west, Manchester people try not to open their teeth when they speak, and further still again, Scousers are just putting it on.

Marsden is a village of a few thousand people – why bother counting them when you can see most of them from the top of Scout Head, the horizon that looks like an Indian Chief laid flat on his back. One of your friends had the name of the village and his birth-date tattooed under his heart but didn't show his mother for two years – it's that combination of rough and smooth. Your parents live here, and the last of your grandparents, and your sister and her family live just down the road in Slaithwaite. Somebody once asked your dad how long a person would have to live in Marsden before they were no longer 'comers-in'. Your dad looked him in the eye and said 'Fifty years, and you'll be dead then.'

Samuel Laycock was born in Marsden. He was a poet. When he was eleven he had some kind of brain dysfunction and moved to Lancashire, ending up in Blackpool for his troubles, but he's remembered in the village in the shape of an up-ended megalith with a square, metal plate bolted to it. The plate bears a small, embossed image of Laycock from the shoulders up, with his balding head, beard and double-breasted jacket, and the words SAMUEL

LAYCOCK, MARSDEN BORN POET. Laycock wrote in Pennine dialect. He was only famous through a handful of towns and villages in the North, but sold thousands of copies of his poems, more than most poets manage to shift throughout the whole country in a lifetime. There's only room for one poet in a village the size of Marsden, which makes Laycock somebody to move past or knock over. The best way to get at him is to take his poems and translate them from whatever version of English he wrote in to whatever version of English you practise yourself. But Laycock died in 1894, so he isn't easily ruffled. He looks out over the bowling green and the tennis court and the bandstand and the flag-pole, his metal face going noticeably greener these last few years – a combination of damp weather and envy.

The Pennine Way comes through Marsden. People who've 'done' the Pennine Way remember Marsden as the place they can't quite remember somewhere near the beginning, or the place they had to get through before they got to the end, somewhere near the end. Marsdeners are known as Cuckoos. They once tried to trap the bird because cuckoos herald the beginning of spring, but to bring a long and not very rewarding narrative to its conclusion, they fucked up. Dimwittedness was the main problem, followed by a poor knowledge of civil-engineering techniques and ignorance of one of the cuckoo's most impressive attributes: the ability to fly. In the next village along the valley, Slaithwaiters are known as Moon Rakers, having tried to drag the reflection of the full moon out of the river. Dimwittedness again played an important part in this legend, though people of that village claim that moon raking was a brilliant and spontaneous alibi given to police when spotted retrieving contraband booze from an underwater hiding place. Slaithwaite, 'Slawitt', is one of the most talked-about, mispronounced place-names in the county, second only, probably, to Penistone.

Marsden has a sheep problem. Last week's *Today's the Day* grand final, hosted by Martyn Lewis on BBC2, showed footage of a village resident impounding a marauding lamb, under an ancient law requiring the shepherd to buy back his stock at market price, or see it sold or eaten. Marsdeners moved closer to their television sets, ready to shout out the name of the village as the correct answer. But the question was about the number of stomachs possessed by that species of creature, and the answer was four.

Colne Valley once had a reputation as a hotbed of radical thought and political activism. It figured strongly in the Luddite uprisings. Enoch Taylor is buried in Marsden, whose looms were pulverized by the hammer of the same name, and William Horsfall was, aptly enough, shot from his horse in Milnsbridge, after saying he'd rather ride up to his saddle girths in blood than give in to the demands of the rabble. Out of the dozens of mills along the valley floor, a handful are still working with wool. The rest are converted into units, full of New Age hippies brewing patchouli oil and making ear-rings out of circuit boards, or moored at the side of the river, rotting away like decommissioned ocean-liners. Weavers' cottages with their double-glazing look down from the hillsides, like old faces wearing new glasses.

In the 1970s, the Valley fell into a long, pleasant afternoon nap. In their sleep, electors stumbled along to voting booths in junior schools and village halls, and put a cross next to the name of Richard Wainwright, Liberal, who held the seat for donkey's years. He was a good man, and that was all anybody needed to know. On your eighteenth birthday he sent you a signed letter on House of Commons stationery welcoming you to the electoral register, and you sold it to your fifteen-year-old friend for ID in the pubs in town. Then in 1987 the unimaginable happened: Graham Riddick, Conservative, was on his way to Westminster. A Union Jack the size of a tea towel hung limply from the 45-degree flag-pole on Marsden Conservative Club. Some quiet demographic revolution had been taking place, and suddenly there were just enough working-class Tories, middle-class snobs, right-wing farmers, upper-class landowners, Pennine businessmen and comers-in to swing things the other way. It should have been expected. The signs were all there. In Sainsbury's car park, domesticated jeeps and people-carriers outnumbered proper cars three to one.

At the next election, with most Conservative MPs hanging on by the width of a credit card, Riddick got in again with an increased majority.

Colne Valley. At junior school you supported Huddersfield Town, 'Town'. You'd been taken to see them by a friend of your dad's, who called jackets 'wind-cheaters' and wore driving gloves in the car. Town had won the First Division Championship three times in a row sometime back in the Stone Age, so there was history, and therefore hope. But because they were crap, you were allowed another team, Leeds, which was where your mother went shopping if she needed an 'outfit' or where you ended up if you didn't get off the train in Town. It was all very simple, until secondary school, when kids from Saddleworth turned up on funny coloured buses, speaking a strange language, wearing red scarfs tied to their wrists and carrying red plastic holdalls with a silhouette of the devil on the side pocket.

You were thirteen when you first went to Old Trafford. Being a Town fan, you'd never seen fifty thousand people gathered together in one lump, and you'd certainly never seen European football. You'd never been to a floodlit match either, and the teams came on to the pitch like Subbuteo men tipped out on a snooker table. This was in the days before supporting Manchester United became like supporting U2 or the Sony Corporation, in the days when you handed cash over the turnstile and walked on to the terrace.

United were playing Juventus, whose goalie, Dino Zoff, was reckoned to be the best in the world at the time. As he trotted out towards the Stretford End where you were standing, a light ripple of applause ran around the ground, and he lifted his arm and held his index finger in the air, to collect the praise and to confirm his status as the world's number one. That was his big mistake. Suddenly he was staring at tens of thousands of outstretched arms, each one carrying a fist or two fingers, and the insults speared at him needed no translation into Italian. Zoff had fallen for the electric handshake. In another sense, in a split second he'd elevated himself from goalkeeper to God, and the crowd were having none of it. For the rest of the match he was a troubled and lonely figure, stood as far away from the crowd as possible, only coming near to pick the ball out of the net.

The next round was against Ajax, in the days when Ajax was still pronounced like a bathroom cleaner. You were in the Scoreboard End. Before the kick-off, a man behind you leant over the barrier and spat a hot wet blob of bubble gum into your hair. Your friend's dad told you to leave it alone, but you messed with it for ninety minutes, and when you got back, you had to have a bald patch hacked into the top of your head to get rid of the chuddie. At school next day, you got battered for saying where you'd been, and battered again for looking like a medieval monk. You can't remember the score, but the net outcome was a defeat.

You went away to college in Portsmouth for three years at the time when the Fleet was setting out for the South Atlantic, and got glassed in the head in a pub for being from Up North and for looking like a sailor. When you came home at Christmas you got punched for going Down South and for saying Malvinas instead of Falklands. If the stitches in the scalp were a kind of 'keep out', then the black eye was a kind of 'welcome home', and you got both messages loud and clear. A couple of months ago, the Vice-Chancellor of Portsmouth University (as it is now) wrote to you asking 'if you would be willing to accept the conferment of the Degree of Doctor of Letters in recognition of your outstanding contribution to the modern poetry movement'. In your dreams, you're congratulated by a professor with a parchment in one hand and a broken Pils bottle behind his back in the other.

You worked for the Probation Service in Manchester for six years, driving round estates looking at bruised children, writing reports on smack-heads who were shooting up in their groin, listening to the coppers in the cells under the courthouse singing 'Police release me let me go'. You once rushed a baby to hospital with a suspected cigarette burn on his chest. The doctor examined the baby and said, 'Where?'

'There,' you said.

'Where?' asked the doctor.

'There,' you said, pointing at the bright red mark on the baby's skin.

'That's his nipple,' said the doctor. 'He's got another one on the other side just like it.'

You worked with one lad who got stabbed in the small of his back trying to swipe a bag of heroin from his dealer. He didn't go to hospital till he was shitting out of the hole, three days later. The son of a woman on your caseload died in an incident involving a bathful of scalding water. They took all your files away for inspection, but you'd done everything by the book. The monstrous bird of guilt circled above the town looking for somewhere to strike, but those out in the open kept their nerve when they stood in the cold of its shadow, and those who could offer it a thick skin or a pair of tight lips to home in on kept well under cover, and it flew off over the red-brick houses, robbed of its kill.

You went to a block of flats once to interview an old woman about something or other, and her Alsatian dog followed you through the door and into the front-room. After about half an hour, the dog got up and crapped in the corner, then sat back down by the fire. At first you thought it was none of your business, but eventually you couldn't keep your mouth shut, and asked her why she didn't make her dog go outside. 'It's not my dog,' she said, 'I thought it was yours.' Actually, that story isn't true, but people told it so many times you started to believe it happened to you.

Another woman you worked with had three kids, massive debts and no money. You went round to her house one day and there was a huge Rottweiler bitch in the kitchen, eating a bucket of food.

'What have you got that for?' you asked the woman.

'Ten quid,' she said.

On another visit the dog wouldn't stop growling at you. 'Don't worry,' the woman said. 'It's because you're drinking out of her cup.' That story isn't true either.

Before you parted company with the Probation Service, you were working as the Bail Intervention Officer at Oldham Magistrates' Court. Every day was different, every day was the same. Every morning at about seven o'clock, you turned up at the police station and, if you remembered the passwords and key-codes, made your way along a concrete tunnel, up a flight of stairs, and emerged in the holding cells under the courtroom. The desk sergeant, if he was in a good mood, gave you a list of the men and women arrested overnight, along with a few details of the offences. If he'd got out of bed on the wrong side, or hadn't been asked to do overtime at Old Trafford for the big match on Saturday, you sat there like a lemon until one of the other officers finished his coffee and threw a bunch of papers at you.

The holding area was a few desks and telephones, iron gates at either end of a long corridor, half a dozen cells to either side, and a glass interview room in the middle, known as the goldfish bowl. Usually, there were five or six men in each cell, in various stages of alertness, ranging from the comatose drunk to the manic junkie. They'd shout through the narrow grille in the metal door until one of the officers put down the newspaper, hauled himself off his chair and strolled over to the cell, his Doc Martens squeaking on the lino floor.

'I'll need a piss, Boss.'

'You've had a piss. Tie a knot in it.'

'Give us a spark, Boss.'

A cigarette comes poking out through the mesh. The officer holds a lighted match just out of reach. 'Say "please".'

'Don't be cunt, Boss. Give us a spark.'

The officer might light the cigarette, or he might not.

'Come on, Boss, I need a piss.'

If he can be bothered the officer opens the door with one of the keys hanging from his belt-loop, and a cloud of Old Holborn billows into the corridor. Bodies come to light at the back of the room: asleep, smoking, doing press-ups, staring, yawning. Someone emerges and the officer marches him to the toilet, waiting outside to walk him back again.

'Come on, get on with it. If you shake it more than twice you're having a wank.'

'Boss, there's no paper.'

'So use your sleeve.'

'Boss, will I get bail, will I?'

'You'll go to hell if it's up to me, but I'm sure this nice gentleman from the Probation Service might sort you out a five-star hotel for a few weeks.'

It was the job of the nice man from the Probation Service to present 'positive, factual, and verified' information to the court that might lead to an offender being bailed to a second appearance, rather than held in custody. At least, that was the written-down version. In reality, he tried to remind the bench that bail was a right, not a privilege, and wanted to impress on them the idea that a shoplifter from Glodwick with a house and a family is more likely to come back to court to face the punishment than flee to a luxury villa in Marbella, beyond the grasp of British justice.

In the goldfish bowl, you ran through a standard list of questions as they called the bodies out of the cells, one at a time. For most of them, you were the first person they'd seen since being nabbed, and after a year or so you reckoned you could fit the character to the crime without asking.

Puke or blood down the front of his shirt, wanting to know the time: Drunk and Disorderly.

Calm and quiet, saying nothing without speaking to a solicitor: Possession with Intent to Supply.

Asking you to phone up and tell her he's sorry: Actual Bodily Harm.

Seventeen, wedge haircut, trainers: Taking without Owner's Consent.

Track marks up the arm, saying that she needs the kids taking to her mother's: Shoplifting.

Eyes on stalks, a muscle throbbing at the back of the jaw, reeling off improbabilities one after another: Illegal Possession of a Controlled Substance.

Alert, mindful, innocent: Indecent Assault.

Terrified, short of breath: Manslaughter.

Silent, heavy, sad: Murder.

Angry, flabbergasted, indignant: Guilty.

Bewildered, tearful, compliant: Guilty.

Stereotypes – a stupid game to play, but there was satisfaction in getting it right and satisfaction in getting it wrong. In any event, it wasn't as if you were judging them by the distance between their eyes. The magistrates did that. Your job was to drive round to a house, knock on a door and wait for someone to come downstairs or open a bedroom window, usually a wife or a mother in a nightdress.

You: 'Mrs So-and-so?'

Her: 'Who wants to know?'

You: 'Probation.'

Her: 'What's he done this time?'

You: 'Nicked a car.'

Her: 'What do you want me to do about it?'

You: 'Is this his address?'

Her: 'I should hope so, he lives here.'

You: 'Is he working?'

Her: 'Yes, he's Managing Director of ICI.'

You: 'OK, thanks.'

Her: 'What time's he up in court?'

You: 'Sometime after ten.'

Her: 'Hang on a minute, I'll come with you.'

There was no natural light in the holding area, only fluorescent strips, and the police worked eight- or nine-hour shifts. They handcuffed prisoners to their own wrists, walked them through the iron gates and upstairs into the courtroom, stood with them in the dock, then dragged them back down to the cells to be carted off to Strangeways. They were known as the pit ponies.

Driving back to West Yorkshire through the cutting every night was a way of shutting the door behind you, watching the *Oldham Metropolitan Borough* sign disappear in the rear-view mirror. Always work away from home. Don't bring dirt to your own doorstep. Always set off to the west in a morning and come back to the east at night – that way you keep the sun out of your eyes. Always live where the rivers run from left to right, like writing.

Your front door opens out on to some of the most empty and dangerous countryside in Britain. Hundreds of square miles of saturated earth and rotting peat, a kind of spongy version of the sea. When you were a kid you walked across the moors looking for dead bodies, but found tractor tyres instead, or fridge-freezers, or crash helmets, miles from anything or anywhere. The only other thing to do was to break into the air shafts above the railway tunnel and drop stones on to the Liverpool train.

At the same time as being remote and away from it all, you're only an hour away from Sheffield, Leeds, Bradford or Manchester, and only one hour forty-three minutes from London on the Electrified East Coast Line, the rail route that's turned Wakefield and Doncaster into commuter towns.

At least, it was one hour forty-three minutes the last time you looked, but the people who own the line this week have probably got together with the people who own the rolling stock, who might have spoken to the cartel who've just bought the signalling system, who could quite possibly have made contact with the catering company and the maintenance contractors, and another couple of minutes might have been sliced off the travelling time. Not that you can moan about covering two hundred miles in less than an hour and three-quarters, but you do get the feeling that a bit more introspection rather than the odd bit of interaction might make things even quicker, and certainly a lot less complicated. And if you need information on connections to trans-Pennine services at this end (those trains that look like buses, with the brake system linked to the door mechanism so that the train won't move if the door isn't water-tight) or one of the lines hooking into London when you get there – tough.

The Electrified East Coast Line is the main artery in a rail network suffering from poor circulation and amputation. At the auction, this was the working part that the latter-day body-snatchers wanted to bid for. The swankiest trains in the country, recently painted a sinister, nuclear-waste-carrying blue, glide up and down between London and Edinburgh, collecting passengers at certain mainline stations, sweeping through others at the speed of thought, leaving a vacuum behind, followed by a hurricane. It's said that Yorkshire prostitutes travel to London on these trains for a week's work in the Big Smoke, and make enough in the toilets on the way down to pay for the ticket. Which particular ticket they prefer hasn't been recorded, because purchasing one is not an easy business given the variety of choice, including Apex, Daypex, SuperAdvance, SuperSaver, Saver, and Standard. A basic tip here is not to head south from these parts before ten o'clock in the morning, or you're looking at a hundred pounds. That is unless you've bought your ticket in London and you're travelling on the return portion, which is what the businessmen and women of Yorkshire do, in which case you can save yourself or your company fifty quid. The highest fares are for the ignorant and those poor souls who go to the capital less than once a month.

There are also rules against travelling on Fridays and travelling north at teatime, just in case you'd wondered about coming home for the weekend. Then there's the question of class. The trains running north–south usually arrive with the First-Class carriages to the front and the Standard-Class to the rear, with a buffet car in the middle as a border point. The smoking carriages are located at the very back – presumably towed on a length of rope. Everyone in Britain knows you can never change your class, but not everyone knows that by taking breakfast in the First-Class restaurant car at Newark, perhaps, or maybe Grantham, you can just about spin out the last corner of toast and the last thimble of marmalade to Welwyn Garden City, by which time you're safe. Breakfast does cost £12.50, and you will be offered black pudding, but it's cheaper than buying the correct ticket, and creates a certain amount of excitement, given that the view out of the window, for most of the way, is Lincolnshire.

There is another category of class, however, which goes under the name of Silver Standard, made up of one or two carriages forming a buffer zone between First and Standard. For a few pounds more than the cheapest fare, you can separate yourself from your fellow commoners and be served with bottomless coffee from Wakefield Westgate to King's Cross. You'll also be furnished with a handkerchief-sized Silver Standard cloth, draped over the headrest, to absorb the sweat or grease from the back of your head and, more importantly, protect the back of your head from the sweat and the grease of previous passengers. On the downside, Silver Standard is always full, because the merchants of the North are falling over each other to distinguish themselves from their kith and kin, especially if it only costs a couple of sovs. In their eighty-twenty suits and Crimplene skirts, the whole carriage humming with static electricity and perspiration, they look down their noses and over the top of their complimentary *Daily Telegraphs* at those pitiful travellers having to fetch their own rust-coloured tea and Sandwich of the Month from the buffet. Back down the line in the cattle trucks, the SuperSavers spread their magazines and books over the tables and put their feet up on the seat opposite.

You live just to the left of where the upright of one great communication corridor slashes the crossbar of another, a good place for going away from and coming back to, a good place for getting the gist. The North, where the M1 does its emergency stop, and away over the back of the hill is the M62, gouged into the moorland and completely out of its element. At one point, the carriageways separate to pass each side of a farm, and a farmer brings his cows for milking at dusk through a subway, into his central reservation. Thousands of tons of steel pass any given point every minute of the day, but when the winter brings the motorway to a frozen standstill, convoys are snuffed out by the snow in less than an hour, and vehicles are excavated weeks later like woolly mammoths out of the tundra. The M62, like a belt drawn tightly across the waistline of Britain, with the buckle somewhere near Leeds.

From the observation suite of Emley Moor Mast, not much short of a thousand feet of fluted concrete with a hypodermic aerial on top, just south of Huddersfield, you can see both coasts. Or you could do, if you were allowed up it and the weather was clear, which you aren't, and even if you were, it wouldn't be. From Castle Hill, the other local landmark, the next highest ground going east are the Ural Mountains in Russia, and you can't see them either.

It's the middle distance really, but you call it the North. The North, where England tucks its shirt in its underpants. It's not all to do with Peter Snow's election map being mainly blue at the bottom and completely red at the top, although that comes into it. And it's more complicated than women wearing rollers and aprons, scrubbing the front step and boil-washing their husbands' shirts, and their husbands pissing in the sink if the wife's on the toilet, and their daughters in snow-washed supermarket jeans and crop-tops eating baked beans straight from the can, and their arm-wrestling sons farting in the one-minute silence at Hillsborough and turning over the mobile Ultra-Burger hot-dog stand after a night on the sauce, although that comes into it as well. The North can also be Lancashire, which is really the North-West, and it can also be Northumberland, which is the North-East, and sometimes it's Humberside, which is the Netherlands, and it can be Cumbria, which is the Lake District, and therefore Scotland. But right here is the North, with its gods and its devils; where Jarvis Cocker meets Geoffrey Boycott, where Emily Brontë meets David Batty, where Ted Hughes meets Darren Gough, where David Hockney meets Peter Sutcliffe, where Brian Glover meets Henry

Moore, and where Bernard Ingham meets Prince Naseem Hamed, or at least if there's any justice he does.

In one sense, it's neither here nor there; land with a line drawn around it for no particular reason, too far-flung to give a single name, too divided into layers and quarters and stripes to think of as whole, too many claims on it to call your own.

But in another sense, it's where you're at, the big piece of the jigsaw. The place between the shoreline and the ridge, between the middle and the rest. The place between the stainless-steel Minotaur keeping guard over Meadowhall, and the kitchen sink; between the Brick Man of Holbeck, who never was, and the Cowthorpe Oak, the country's oldest living thing, which is no more. The place between the fifty-foot drifts of '47, and last year's reservoirs backed into dust-bowls and craters of the moon; between cotton-grass bleaching its hair on White Moss, and a bird's-eye view of the Humber Bridge. Between the rocking stone at Brandreth Crags and the last pebble on Spurn Point; between the red deer and the pygmy shrew; between the four-lane stretch from Junction 25 to Ainley Top, and the Lyke Wake Walk. The place between the male-voice choir, and the Western Terrace singing this year's chant on the first day of the Headingley Test; the Goldcrest, and the bones of elephants and big cats in Kirkdale cave; the secret Lady's Slipper orchid, and the burning of the saints; Good Friday's Pace Egg Play, and open season on 1st April. The place between Kilnsea and Lower Bentham, Totley and Staithes; between Bangladesh and Bradford Interchange; between the flea with its teeth in anything that moves, and the magpie with its charm; Halifax PLC, and the worst busker in Leeds without a penny to scratch his arse. Between the fly who'll drink with anyone, and the side of bacon – better when hung; between those lying dead in their graves like cargo lost from the shipwreck of Heptonstall Church, and those coming back from the sea with their lives into Grimsby and Hull;

between the aerials and masts decoding babble and gibberish out of the air, and the deep, cathedral quiet of Gaping Gill, three hundred feet below ground; between the rocks in the cairns on the tops of the hills, and the hard places down in the seven cities and hundred towns.

It's halfway to heaven, they reckon, here in the county with more acres than letters in the Bible. It's the distance between, the difference of this from the next, one from another. And you, you live on the border.

*

Late News: Last week, the word *Lancashire* was daubed in red paint across the Saddleworth sign and its white rose. It isn't clear if the action was taken by people on this side of the hill who've turned against their former county-folk, or people from the far side, who've thrown in the towel.

A Place to Call Home

Driving around looking for a house to buy, you stray over the top into Lancashire, and call in at a friend's farm in Strinesdale, only to find that it's been the site of a terrible tragedy. During last night's thunderstorms, forked lightning hit the paddock in front of the house, and the cow that was grazing there was killed. It lies in a big black heap by the gate, steaming in this morning's sun, at the end of a long muddy streak where Roy towed it back from the field with the JCB. The cow was in calf, and a bullock in the same field – last year's offspring – mopes and mooches at the top of the hill, refusing to come into the barn. Waiting for the knackers, Roy tells you that for some reason cows are more susceptible to lightning strikes than horses, which surprises you, not just because horses are taller and therefore a more obvious target, but because they wear metal shoes. You also wonder how much the statistics for this kind of thing have been skewed by foul play, remembering what a vet once told you. During his career he said he'd been called to umpteen farms where cows had been 'struck by lightning', only to find a diseased corpse at the end of a pair of tyre tracks, dumped beneath a burnt tree with the smell of petrol still in the air. Cows killed by acts of God qualify for insurance money, and can also be sold to the abattoir for meatstuffs.

Not that foul play is a possibility in this case. Roy retired from a job in the city last year, and all the animals on the farm are pets really, with names and collars around their necks. You can see that he's genuinely upset and anxious about the dead cow, but at

19

the same time there's a kind of excitement in his face, as if something truly agricultural has happened, making him a proper farmer for the first time, not just a retired businessman with a smallholding on the outskirts of Oldham. You drive back over the border, across the motorway bridge at Scammonden, thinking about Roy in the JCB, scooping the cow up in the bucket and tipping its great stiffening mass into the knacker's van, watching it trundle down the lane.

The next house on the list is in a quiet wooded valley in Calderdale not far from the M62 and on the right side of the county boundary. The property is one-third of an old mill-owner's house, miles too big and miles too expensive, but the estate agent was adamant that you looked at it, and you park at the top of the drive and walk down through a walled garden, between two lines of monkey puzzle trees. The couple who own it are in their mid thirties with a two-year-old girl and another on the way. 'We're moving nearer town,' says Morag, in a Scottish accent infiltrated by Yorkshire vowels. 'Jim gets called into work so much, it's silly not be nearer.'

Visits to houses nearly always start with the vendors supplying this kind of information, giving a legitimate reason for leaving, rather than letting on about the poltergeist that refuses to budge despite exorcisms from the Bishop of Wakefield, or plans that were recently passed for the siting of a glue factory and tannery in the next field. Another experience common to house-hunters in Calderdale is to find that the property usually hosts an electricity pylon in the back garden, and that a thousand-megavolt power line passes within spitting distance of the front bedroom. Rather than drive around the area looking for For Sale boards, buyers are better advised to follow the miles of thick grey cables, or look for the pylons that hold them, like a tug-of-war team holding their ground against the next village. All the decent houses are directly beneath.

At Valley Ford House there is no pylon, but there must be a

power station nearby to supply all the various gadgets and gizmos in the place, beginning with the music system. Jim slides back the cover of a cabinet in the living-room, revealing something like the instrument panel of the space shuttle, and talks you through the various knobs and dials, assuring you of its value and reminding you that they won't be taking it with them when they move. In every room, Morag reels off the thickness of the carpet and the depth of the alcoves. Then Jim steps in with a handset, points it at a flashing panel somewhere in the ceiling, and the sound of Luther Vandross on CD or Danny Baker on Radio 1 or Richard and Judy on daytime television rises and falls as he runs his thumb up and down the volume control.

'We thought the wardrobes were MFI, so we were going to chuck them,' says Morag in the bedroom, 'but it turned out they're Strachan, so we left them in, obviously.' She carries on into the *en suite* bathroom, pointing out the shower unit with the wooden seat, the heated towel rail, the oval jacuzzi and the low-flush toilet and bidet, until she reaches the window at the far end. 'And this is the window,' she says, then nods at Jim, who draws his handset from its holster, and Elton John ricochets between the hand-painted tiles and the full-length mirrors.

Downstairs, you're led into a drawing-room with a red carpet, red walls and a red ceiling, reminiscent of the surgeon's room on HMS *Victory*, painted that colour to disguise the blood. 'We call it the red room. Jim, pull the shutters to show how dark it is.' Jim closes the wooden shutters on the two windows, and we stand there in the pitch black, with only the pulsing of a tiny red light in the sensor panel above us, like a distant star. In the kitchen, there's an ornate wood-burning stove, like a green postbox, in the fireplace. 'Does it draw?' you ask her.

'Excuse me?'

'Does it draw the smoke and keep the fire going?'

'Oh', she says, 'actually we've never had it lit.'

In every room there's a mobile phone charging in a socket, and so many pieces of communication equipment such as faxes and modems and answerphones that you wonder why Jim has to go to work at all, let alone move closer to it. The finale of the tour takes place in a cupboard under the stairs, where Jim demonstrates a telephone exchange that could probably facilitate the Yorkshire Water complaints department, with lines to spare. At one moment, he turns to you and says, 'But the great beauty of this system is that you can block your guests from making international phone calls.' You picture your mum and dad, staying over one night, surreptitiously lifting the receiver at three in the morning, foiled in their efforts to get through to Montevideo or Karachi. You think of the plastic telephone/address book you once bought them with the sliding catch and the pop-up cover, wondering if it actually contains a single number for someone in another country.

House-hunting in Farnley Tyas, one of Huddersfield's most sought-after outlying villages, and probably most burgled. Sandra, going out to Durban with her husband's job, shows you the fitted kitchen. 'This is the griddle, this is the hob, this is the fan-assisted oven – you should knock half an hour off your meat with that – and this is the turbo grill, for barbecue chicken. Have you tried barbecue chicken? It's very tasty.' The dining table is a slab of granite, part of the bedrock that the house must have been built around. Framed in the bathroom window, Emley Moor Mast, like the after-burn of a rocket disappearing into the clouds. In the children's bedroom, she's stuck luminous stars to the walls and ceiling in their correct celestial positions. 'When I'm stressed, I lie down in here, turn out the lights and pretend I'm outside.' She flops back on to the bed and laughs, kicks her legs in the air, with the Mr Moon and Mr Sun wall-lamps beaming at each side of her, under the constellation of Cygnus the Swan.

House-hunting in Luddenden Foot, or Clubbenden Foot, as it's known. You follow directions down an unmade road to the cottage, where there are already five or six cars parked alongside the garden fence. Inside, the estate agent's representative is showing a handful of prospective buyers around the house, but as soon as you step over the threshold you become one of half a dozen disinterested parties. Clothes are strewn on the floor of every room, knickers and socks are erupting from every drawer, boxes of batteries and videos are tipped out on to a table, washing-up festers in the sink, children's toys – most of them broken – are herded into corners, and spores of talcum powder are still filtering through the air. It looks and feels as if some unmentionable practice had been going on over a number of years, which came to an end this morning, just an hour or so before the police arrived and turned the place over. A woman in a blue dress comes out of a bedroom with a handkerchief over her mouth. People pass each other at the head of the stairs and grimace, silently. Nobody dares look in the bathroom. Through the window, the 'rock-pool' in the garden is a puddle of piss-coloured water on a sheet of tarpaulin, covering who knows what. Everywhere the smell of damp, like a dungeon.

You go outside for some fresh air and see that the gable-end of the house is built into a banking, which then rises steeply above the roof. More than that, it's as if the house is retaining the hillside, shouldering the moor, shoring up the whole of the Pennines which are ready now to slump into the valley bottom, roll over like an animal on to its back, burying the abandoned cottage and all of the evidence.

House-hunting in Holmfirth. You're shown around a three-storey Victorian house by Mrs Micklethwaite, who finally leads you up to the attic to point out the two rooms in the roof space. She walks to the far wall, towards a tiny door with a wooden handle, saying, 'And this is just a cubby-hole, really.' Inside the room, which is about six-feet square and without a window, three sons and their father are huddled around a computer screen, playing a video game. The father, his eyes fixed to the screen, raises the back of his hand towards you, which you take to be the 'Hello' of a man who doesn't want to be disturbed. Thinking about it afterwards, you can see that it also meant 'silence', and 'halt', and 'goodbye'.

King Arthur in the East Riding

And if they go away from home, their reason is equally cogent: 'What does it signify how we dress here, where nobody knows us?' – Mrs Gaskell, *Cranford*

We must look like a pretty odd collection of people, the ninety of us gathered by the lych-gate with suitcases and bags at half-nine on a Saturday morning. One man cracks open a can of beer and his wife shakes her head in despair. A woman in a spangly gold blouse and leggings pours tea from a flask and offers the cup round. A couple come out of a house across the road and join the rest of us, talking about the weather and looking at our watches. When the two coaches arrive, we load the bags and cases into the big black cave of each boot, and the drivers in their short-sleeved white shirts with black epaulettes share a cigarette, one of them flicking the smouldering dimp into the river. Someone scurries about with a clipboard ticking off names from a list: Muskett, Haig, Carter, Howarth, Norcliffe, Armitage, Byrom, Lodge, Hall, Hoyle, Dyson, Schorthorn, Whitehead, Kewley – we couldn't really be from anywhere else other than West Yorkshire.

The wagon turns up, full to the back with props, costumes and scenery, and the driver sounds the horn a couple of times making a noise like an American freight train, leading the convoy up Peel Street and out of the village.

We're a mixed bunch, there's no doubt about that, with very different ideas about what to wear for a weekend in Bridlington at the end of April. For some people it's jeans, trainers and a T-shirt, for others it's a heavy woollen suit with braces and brogues, and for those of us who've spent any time on Yorkshire's east coast, it's a thick jumper with a waterproof coat in reserve. Most of us talk louder than we need to about which guesthouse we're staying in, how we're going to kill time before the evening, whether or not we've remembered to pack everything we need. The coach stops a couple more times along the main road to pick up the handful of people who don't actually live in the village, then on into Huddersfield. Past the derelict façade of Ivanhoe's nightclub where the Sex Pistols played their last British gig – the gig that you always say you went to, but didn't. Past the McAlpine Stadium, Huddersfield Town's relocated ground looking like a blue and white lunar module – enough of a stadium to host the likes of REM and Oasis last year, and some half-decent football matches as well. Past the scrapyard where Peter Sutcliffe bought his false number-plates, and then we're chugging up the slip road and on to the motorway.

The man in front of me studies the racing pages of the *Yorkshire Post*. The man in front of him shouts out crossword clues from the *Guardian*. The man in front of him can't wait a minute longer, and unpacks a steaming bacon butty from a parcel of silver foil. In front of him, two men go through a script together, rehearsing lines.

'I'd give you a peck on the cheek, but I've got scruples.'

'Don't worry, Lancelot, I've already had them.'

'I shall seal our love with a kiss.'

'I'm hoping we can seal it a lot tighter than that!'

'Guinevere, I love you. I shall kiss you on the lips or bust.'

'Well make your mind up!'

And so on. On the M62 the coaches and the wagon overtake each other, which brings about a variety of hand signals and gestures, ranging from a royal wave to an up-and-down movement of the thumb and index finger in the shape of a circle, mainly between the men towards the back end of each coach. The wagon driver pomps the horn again as we overtake him up the hill out of Brighouse. Further along, we pass two double-deckers doing fifty on the inside lane, the first one full of Asian women sitting downstairs, the second full of Asian men sitting upstairs, both buses painted orange and turquoise. We wave, and they wave back. 'Wedding job,' someone says, and everyone agrees.

Further east, on the section of the motorway that becomes straight and quiet like a runway, we turn off at the Goole exit along a road running between two fields of sugar beet, before pulling on to the gravel forecourt of a truck stop, the bus bottoming on the uneven surface of pot-holes and puddles.

'Greasy Spoon,' somebody moans.

'It's a road-house,' his wife corrects him. 'I'll have tea and an orange Kit-Kat.'

Whatever the Redbeck Café is or isn't, the six or seven customers inside are slightly bemused when we all pile in, and a man in an orange Railtrack diddy-jacket puts on his glasses to watch us forming an orderly but noisy queue between the formica tables and the video games. A lorry driver pumps money into a slot-machine in the far corner that plays *The Star Spangled Banner* every time it spits out a ten-pence piece. A couple with two children smoke without speaking to each other, while their kids lick their fingers and draw on the table with ash from the ashtray. In our party, the hungriest push to the front to order the breakfast special, a slimy mound of bacon, eggs, mushrooms, sausage, beans, fried bread and tomatoes, covered over with a helping of chips. £2.30. The rest of us stand for twenty minutes, soaking up the cigarette smoke and the hot fat in the air, reading the 'Missing, Can-U-Help' posters of long-lost teenagers and watching Monster Truck Racing on the telly bolted to the wall. You're sent by some of the women to check out the toilets, and walk down a long corridor with battered shower units to the left with wooden pallets on the floor to stand on. You're expecting the loos at the far end to be slarted with the shit of a thousand lorry-driving arses, but they're clean and shiny, with dozens of toilet rolls stashed behind the flush-pipe like rounds of ammunition. You give the thumbs up, and the women set off down the dark corridor towards the cubicles, in pairs.

Most people have taken their drinks outside and are sitting on a concrete wall with the sun just beginning to break through. A twelve-wheeler spins out of the car park throwing up a small grey cloud of dust, and some of the men look on admiringly. A woman feeds the last bit of a sausage sandwich to a dog through a half-opened car window, and shrieks when it wolfs down the paper plate as well. Your mum comes outside with red cheeks and tears rolling down her face. 'Swallowed a crumb,' she manages to croak, and someone slaps her hard between the shoulder-blades until she coughs it out. Your dad lights his pipe and blows the smoke through his teeth with his head back, looking at the sky. Then he turns around and sees you watching him, and winks. You nod your head. Then the wagon driver gives one long pull on the horn, like the klaxon at the end of a Rugby League match, and we climb back on the buses, some people wiping the grease from their lips on the back of their hands, some people spilling coffee from styrofoam cups as we wobble out of the car park on to the road. The next twenty or thirty miles are a steady cruise between fields of potatoes with scarecrows crucified left, right and centre, and past hundreds of pigs, sunning themselves outside their own cut-down Anderson shelters.

As we get near the edge of town, there's growing excitement on the coach. People stand up to get a better view, even though there's nothing to see. Nearly everyone in West Yorkshire has been to 'Brid' on holiday at some time in their life, just like nearly everyone in Lancashire has been to Blackpool, and there's a great deal of this-is-where-so-and-so-happened or isn't-that-where-what's-his-face-did-such-and-such, before we turn off the High Street into avenues where every house has a B&B sign outside and a 'Vacancies' notice in the window.

At the front of the bus, someone pipes up, 'This is like going to Wembley,' which is a nice idea but not really a fair comparison. Amateur footballers probably dream of the twin towers every night, but nobody at Pule Side Working Men's Club ever had any real desire to perform their all-male panto anywhere other than the village hall. When the Northern Operatic and Dramatic Association asked us to take the production to their annual conference, at the thousand-seater Spa Theatre, it was such a pie-in-the-sky and off-the-wall and out-of-the-blue idea that nobody really knew what it was we'd agreed to. But that was six months ago, and today's the day, and tonight's the night, and it's a big deal. The bus draws up alongside four landladies having a chin-wag on the pavement; we're taken off to our guesthouses, all within fifty yards and facing each other. There are more hand signals and gestures across the street from those of us with rooms at the front.

Although Bridlington's gone the way of most seaside towns during the last twenty years, it still has its self-respect. It might be one of England's deteriorating coastal resorts, but it also has the feel of a place where people live and work, even if it isn't clear what they do. We walk through what might well be the rough end of town, past a butcher's with meat going grey in the window, past half a dozen charity shops selling socks from plastic dustbins at £3.99 for five pairs, and another with pac-a-macs, acrylic 'ganseys' and brown polyester 'slacks' hung up on the outside of the window. In the town centre, four of us call at an ice-cream parlour for a knickerbocker glory, something you were never allowed when you came here on holiday. Segments of tinned fruit sink like slugs to the bottom of a glass chalice where molten ice-cream curdles with half an inch of raspberry-coloured chemicals. It's disgusting, and we end up catapulting pineapple chunks at each other with the long-handled spoons. We're also disappointed to see that it isn't even the most expensive item, and that for another thirty pence we could have gone the whole hog with an ice-cream sundae, any flavour.

Everyone's split up now, and we keep bumping into various branches of the tribe along the prom and on the harbour. Muskett goes past with a fried haddock hanging from his mouth, unable to speak. The Whitehead sisters have just bought two Supa-Soaka pump-action water pistols for their kids, and grin as they go by sharing the ear-plugs of the same Walkman, mouthing the words of the same song.

You're gawping into a shop, 'Hilda's', that has twelve pairs of enormous white knickers laid out in the window without price or explanation, when your mum taps you on the back. 'Enjoying yourself?'

'Yeah. Where's Dad?'

She points in the direction of the Spa. 'He's on pins. He's gone for a snoop.'

I can see him walking along the front towards the theatre, pipe smoke curling over his shoulder.

'You know what he's like,' she says. 'See you later.'

She marches off up the street to join him, and you watch him pointing out some feature on the big grey building in front of them with the glass cupola. They're looking at the zipper sign on the side of the theatre, with the moving message advertising tonight's performance in electric-red letters.

If he is more nervous than the rest of us, then he's probably got every right to be. For one thing, he wrote the pantomime, and for another, he's the producer. No matter how much any one else is involved, it's all down to him in the end. Not only that, he's putting himself on the line in front of his friends and colleagues from the strange world of amateur dramatics, and putting his faith in a bunch of blokes whose common bond has nothing to do with acting or singing and everything to do with the club where they go drinking. He's slapped a 'no getting pissed' order on the cast, but given that we don't go on stage till midnight, the chances of it holding are pretty non-existent. He walks on towards the theatre with my mum, and another puff of tobacco smoke rises up into the ether.

To pass the time, we walk along the cliff path to Sewerby, the better end of Bridlington, despite what the first two syllables of its name might suggest. We pay for a game of crown green bowls, but because our footwear is 'too clumpy' we're invited to wear a pair of overshoes – rubber heels with straps, like the back half of a black sandal, or something given to a child with one leg shorter than the other. The green-keeper fishes them out of a big cardboard box that looks as if it might have gas masks in the bottom as well. We waddle around on the green for an hour in our surgical appliances, taking great divots out of the turf every time we trip up, then wander back towards the town, past the profoundly sad or blissfully contented donkeys carrying children backwards and forwards along the cliff-top for fifty pence a go.

Having dragged its heels all afternoon, the day suddenly begins picking up pace, gaining momentum towards midnight. At six o'clock we're eating a curry in Bridlington's best Indian restaurant. Someone's written 'Very fantastic' in the visitors' book. Five minutes later, at seven o'clock, we're striding down North Marine Drive in black jackets and white shirts, five of us, like the beginning of *Reservoir Dogs*. Nobody says so, but somebody whistles the tune. Ten more seconds and it's half-eight, and we're sitting in the back five rows of the stalls watching the 'other' show, Whitby

Operatics singing a London Medley in cod cockney accents, followed by a selection of songs and routines from *Oklahoma* to *Oliver*, with no apparent connection. During the wedding scene from *Fiddler on the Roof*, the groom's father sings the line 'When did he get to be so tall?' and looks proudly towards his son, who just happens to be the smallest man on the stage by a good six inches. Half the people in the audience implode with convulsions of suppressed laughter, and the other half laugh out loud. Fortunately, the man himself sees the funny side of it, and even from where we're sitting we can see that he's smiling. We're generous with our applause because we know that in three hours' time they'll be part of the audience listening to us, but privately we're glad it's nothing better than pretty good. You can hear your dad thinking, 'It's not a competition, but we can win it.'

During the half an hour it takes Whitby to clear the stage and dressing-rooms, we go for a drink in the ballroom, and find out there's been a bit of 'afters' between some of our contingent in the balcony and a man who whooped and wolf-whistled and made other animal noises during the concert. He's been asked politely at least three times, apparently, but not to any effect, and as a consequence, somebody has followed him into the toilets to 'have a word'. No one asks which particular word it is, but when our man comes back to the bar readjusting his tie and straightening his cuffs, that's the end of the matter.

Eventually, finally, we're allowed backstage, and clamber up through the orchestra pit and look out into the empty auditorium. It might not be the Albert Hall, but it makes Marsden Parochial Hall look like a doll's house. Somebody shouts, 'Hello,' and the word disappears into the gloom beyond the front of the balcony. Spotlights clunk into action somewhere up in the gods, blinding us all for a minute. Just when we're on the verge of wondering what the hell we're doing, doors swing open at the side of the stage and the wagon backs up to the entrance. For the next half an hour we haul boxes and crates and cases and bags into the wings, stretchering rails of clothes to far-away dressing-rooms, hooking curtains and batons to cables and ropes that hoik them upwards into the rafters, marking the floor with chalk and gaffer-tape, then dragging great blocks of scenery juddering into position. Green, yellow and purple lights flood the stage, and the lighting-crew strut around wearing microphone headsets, like air-traffic controllers.

Dad stands in front of the stage, about five rows back, bawling orders at everyone and checking his watch. At about half-eleven, when it looks like we might have time for a bit of a rehearsal, there's a technical hitch, and we have to make do with singing a couple of songs and speeding through a few pages of dialogue. At quarter to twelve, from behind the closed curtain, we can hear the chattering and chunnering of a thousand am-dram snobs from all over the North – big women in glittery backless dresses and mock-croc stilettos, small cigar-smoking men in white tuxedos with long-service medals pinned to their breast pockets – all fingering the makeshift programme that one of us slipped through the office photocopier during a fire alarm.

At five to twelve, most of us are lined up in a corridor outside the make-up room, not saying much. King Arthur blots his lipstick on a napkin, and Merlin clamps his stick-on beard to his chin. One of the fairies asks one of the knights to do up his dress at the back, and another fairy stuffs a third pair of socks into his bra. A man who has only ever been seen with a pint glass in his hand takes a long slug from a bottle of mineral water. A bottle of Johnny Walker Black Label gets passed around, but no one has more than a toothful. Over the intercom we can hear the audience applauding the orchestra – two pianists and the village barber on drums – then a few seconds' pause before the first bars of the overture. Dad calls us all on to stage as if he's about to give a team talk or make some big speech, but he just says 'Enjoy it,' and disappears. We line up across the stage in darkness, and then silence, and stare at the thick red curtain in front of our faces, until it flies open.

From out there it must look very weird, even for a pantomime. We range in height from five-foot-nothing to six-foot-five. In age, from fourteen to sixty-odd. In weight, probably from around eight stone, soaking wet, to something approaching twenty, with those at the top end carrying a lot of it just above the belt. Maybe this wouldn't be so unusual if all the various bodies weren't squeezed into tights, leggings, tutus, tabards, smocks and capes, and if the faces and heads above them weren't caked in panstick and crowned with wigs, smurf hats or tiaras. No one's ever asked why it's an all-male performance, which is just as well because nobody really knows, and it must be obvious by the time we've barked through the first number that no one's expecting red roses at the stage door, or a recording contract, or an audition in the West End.

There's a split second at the end of the song when nothing happens, a hard silence, in which every one of us on stage must wonder if the audience have taken it the wrong way, if they haven't 'approved', if they haven't 'got it'. But it is only a split second, and then an avalanche of clattering applause follows us off the stage and into the dressing-room, to jump into the next robe or frock or chain-mail tank-top and get back out under the lights.

Enjoy it. And we do. From when Arthur yanks the plywood sword from the papier mâché stone to an hour later when, in an unexpected twist to the legend of Camelot, Merlin plugs him with a Second World War revolver, turning to the audience and saying 'Well, he wasn't up to the job.'

During the finale, the stage staff sidle on to stage, followed by your dad in a dinner jacket and bow tie. Even through the darkness at the back of the hall, it's possible to see everybody in the balcony stood up and cheering, waving their programmes, and he stands with his hands behind his back, leaning forward into the applause as if it were sunlight on his face.

The curtains sweep across, and that's it. In one of the dressing-rooms there's a scrum for the only bar of soap as thirty of us try to wash in one bowl of lukewarm water, like hippos round the last muddy puddle at the water hole, and in five minutes we're striding back up the promenade, ready for a drink. It's two in the morning.

No one can really remember how it went, but it doesn't matter, because in the private bar of the Mon Fort Hotel we go through the whole damn thing again, song by song, eighty or ninety of us now, plus three or four bewildered residents in the corner, smiling nervously. At one stage, a drunk in a lumberjack jacket comes in from the street and wanders over to the buffet table, and has to be given 'the Scarborough warning'. I don't know what the Scarborough warning is, exactly; a lot of the men have just had their fiftieth birthdays, which makes them part of the baby-boom generation, and every now and again they fall into a kind of armed-forces lingo which probably came from their fathers. What-ever it is, it works, and the lumberjack returns to his seat outside on the pavement, staring at the seafood vol-au-vents and tandoori chicken drumsticks through one of the bottom panes in the bay window.

Nights like these never end. Whatever time you decide to pack it in, there's always somebody at the bar buying another round, and always somebody at breakfast saying how the landlord went to bed and told everybody to put their money in the till. It's more a question of selecting your own personal point of exit – like jumping off a merry-go-round that never stops – and just before the sun comes up, half a dozen of us spill out on to the road and amble back to the B&B through a cold sea-fret, ready for the end of the day. Four hours later, there's a full English breakfast for those who can manage one, and tea and dry toast for those who can't, served in a mock Tudor dining-room which also incorporates a Scottish theme, including a tartan carpet, a St Andrews golf ball cruet set, a framed photograph of a Highland Terrier wearing a sporran round its neck, and a set of bagpipes nailed to the wall above the bar like a Loch Ness octopus. Somebody rattles paracetamol like dice in a tumbler, and everybody wants one. Eventually we all stumble out of the guesthouse into the sunshine, dragging suitcases and bags on to the pavement, and the coaches arrive. Some of the party from the B&B across the road have started drinking again – either that, or they never stopped – and we fill the street, pointing at one another and laughing, saying how great it was, going on about it.

Riding home, we loll about on the back seat telling stories about school. How Mrs Dyson made Terry Pamment piss his britches by saying, 'You *can* go to the toilet, but you *may* not.' How Jumbo Ellis and his mates broke into the school, and Ellis got stuck in the window, trapping them all inside like a cork.

'He was ginormous,' says someone.

'He's dead,' says someone else.

How a fifth-former threw half a dozen hens into the school one night, followed by a fox.

'That true?'

'Nope,' says the person telling the story.

All the way down the bus, people fall asleep against the windows, their faces and hair squashed flat, leaving big greasy smudges on the glass. We arrive at the church gates, tired and a little bit sunburnt, telling each other we can't decide if it feels like a lifetime ago or no time at all. The old people in the flats across the road stare out of their windows at us, wondering if it was this morning when they saw us loading suitcases into the back of the bus, or possibly yesterday, or maybe the week before last. Everyone sets off walking home, slowly, traces of lipstick still colouring their mouths, stubble growing out through a hint of rouge, mascara hiding the sleep in their eyes.

News Just In

Look North: There's growing concern amongst animal rights campaigners amid increased evidence of quail fighting in the region. The following report contains pictures which some viewers may find disturbing.

On a grainy black-and-white home video, two moth-eaten quails circle each other on the floor of an empty living-room somewhere in West Yorkshire. Apparently the birds are starved for a fortnight, then fed on seed stewed in alcohol, and spurs are clipped to the back of their legs. About the shape and size of a pair of light bulbs or Orangina bottles, they lunge at each other like two men with their hands tied behind their backs, and tiny feathers float up into the air. A man shuffles about on the underlay in the background, waving his arms and pointing, and the action takes place in the coliseum of a fifties tiled fireplace and matching hearth. The sport happens to be very popular in the Middle East, although here in Yorkshire no money ever changes hands on the outcome of a bout – it's purely for fun.

Me, You, and a Dog Named Boo

You go to A&M Records to see them about writing some songs. They've been along, incognito, to one of your readings, and reckon you're the right man to 'put lyricism back into lyrics'. You get a taxi from King's Cross, thinking that the address must be close by, thinking that Sting and Chris de Burgh wouldn't want to go hacking around South London to sign contracts and pick up lorry-loads of cash. But you're practically in Portsmouth by the time you get there, somewhere near Putney Bridge. The Irish girl at reception juggles telephones and flirts with two men in plastic trousers leaning over the desk, speaking a sort of transatlantic cockney. A motorcycle courier comes in with one letter in his leather glove, stands there for five minutes without lifting his visor, then eventually tosses the letter into a wicker basket and leaves.

It's become pretty clear by now that unless you suddenly rip off your mask and reveal yourself to be David Bowie, you're going to have to make something happen. But at the same time you don't want her to think that you're some creepy no-hoper with two dozen demo tapes in a carrier bag and a thousand more in the wardrobe at home. You mumble something to her about the man you've come to see (you call him Bosman, even though you know this is a Belgian footballer and not his name), and after another five minutes or so she announces over the tannoy that 'Mike Armitage is in reception.' You think that she's confused you with the England cricket captain but still managed to get it wrong. Not long afterwards, she leans over the desk and says, 'Steven, you can go upstairs and meet the man.'

You sit on a blue settee, next to another blue settee at right angles. In a quiet moment, you stroll over to the far side of 'the man's' office to look at a photograph of Ilie Nastase, which turns out to be Bryan Ferry at his most unshaven. In the bottom corner he's written 'To Boz – for hiring and firing!' When Boz walks in, he's tall, good-looking, Turkish maybe but ultimately Californian, whatever that means. He's wearing jeans and a plain T-shirt, which you take as a reasonably good sign, and he slides on to the other settee, so you have to turn inwards to look at him. This makes your trouser leg ride up above the top of your sock, offering him a couple of inches of white hairy skin.

Twenty minutes later, you still haven't said hello, and Boz is halfway through his career portfolio to date, beginning somewhere in the seventies during the oil crisis, through Silicon Valley and the computer explosion of the eighties, and eventually to this two-sofa office on the New King's Road. The gist of it is that he's either made a big splash or saved an industry from certain death every time he's put his mind to it, then jumped ship whenever he's sensed a gap in the market or a business opportunity.

You're just about to ask your first question when he begins his second monologue – a lecture on pop music – beginning in 1977 with the extinction of the Rock 'n' Roll Dinosaur. A picture of a long-haired, leather-jacketed Bryan Adams sneers from the wall. Even though Boz only comes up for air between paragraphs, you can tell that you make him nervous, and he begins stretching his vocabulary beyond its operational capabilities. At one point, he finds himself speaking about 'maximal influxions'. Five minutes further on, he's talking about 'timbre' as though it were something a lumberjack might shout, and looks quickly over to you for advice on pronunciation. For some reason, you don't seem able to help him, and give him a well-what's-a-bit-of-pronunciation-between-us-blokes look. Reassured, he carries on towards the outer reaches of the English language.

You're probably embarrassed that he feels he has to speak to you as if you're Andrew Marvell. At the same time you're annoyed, in the way that geography graduates are annoyed when someone asks them, 'So what's the capital of Outer Mongolia, then?', or the way that psychologists are annoyed when accused of analysing people. You're also pissed off with him for saying so many things that you disagree with, and pissed off with yourself for agreeing with him. You can see yourself from where the two Bryans look out from their photographs, nodding like a toy dog.

'And then in 1984 . . .' you hear him saying, while someone in the next office picks up a guitar and murders the first three chords of *Teenage Kicks*.

'So what did you study?' he asks you, noticing that you're drifting out of orbit. 'Geography, then Psychology,' you tell him, expecting your next two answers to be 'Ulan Bator' and 'Would I do that?' But there's obviously no time for idle chit-chat, and pretty soon he's well into his definition of 'the pop lyric' – what it is and what it isn't, and how you might fit into the scheme of things. What it is, apparently, is the subtle, barely noticeable juxtaposition of opposites, such as bitter and sweet, happy and sad. That's all there is to it. What it isn't, apparently, is 'Me, you, and a dog named Boo.' He uses this example several times, to the point where you begin to think how catchy it is, how the barely noticeable juxtaposition of its opposites brings about a kind of bitter/sweet, happy/sad sort of effect.

As you're thinking all this, you're hypnotized by the way he moves to the sound of his own voice, or the way he gives physical expression to his own words by use of his hands, mainly to explain musical terms as he understands them. 'Syncopation', for example, is a kind of two-handed separation, the kind that would cause a squeeze-box to draw breath, or a technique for the stretching of dough during bread-making. 'Harmony' is both hands flat out in front, rising and falling like the levels of a graphic equalizer, and 'melody' is one finger drawing the troughs and peaks of a cable strung out along telegraph poles. During this simultaneous signing (you begin wondering if he has to deal with a lot of deaf people) Boz explains that many of his new acts, while being completely computer literate and speaking music as a first language, when it comes to words and meaning are somewhat . . . 'Challenged?' you suggest. 'Challenged. Exactly.' It therefore follows, apparently, that if they could knock out a few tunes, you could knock out a few verses to go with them. Before you know what you're doing, you're nodding in agreement again, and Ferry and Adams are smirking at each other across the room. 'Of course, I'm sure that writing lyrics will be just the same as writing poetry, only different,' says the man. 'Like wanking with the other hand,' says you. 'Oh, if it was going to be that difficult we wouldn't be asking you to do it,' says he, and a minute later you're back out on the New King's Road in the rain, looking for the tube station. You know for a fact that nothing will come of this, and you guess Boz knows it too. You're soaked to the skin, and a twenty-quid taxi ride down on the deal already.

The Beast and the Flood

One stand-pipe maketh not a summer – Yorkshire Proverb

There's growing evidence for the concept of an oscillating universe, based on a recurring event in West Yorkshire. Every six months or so, a kid on a housing estate climbs over a wall to retrieve a football, and is savaged by a dangerous dog. *Look North* dispatch a film crew to the scene of the crime, to interview the grieving parents and the owner of the dog, usually through a letterbox. A dog breeder then testifies to the gentleness of the breed as a whole, and the piece concludes with news of the destruction of the offending animal. Details vary, but essentially all incidents of this type are the same.

In tonight's version, 'little Michael Swain' has been mauled by next door's bull mastiff. Shot of a framed photograph of Michael in school uniform, shot of scabby leather football rocking innocently on the concrete patio, shot of the exterior of the Swain residence. Inside the house, Mr Swain senior describes the attack, referring on two occasions to the flesh on his son's face as 'meat', and explaining how the flap of his cheek lifted up 'like an envelope'. In the next scene, a breeder from somewhere else in the region defends the good name of the bull mastiff, while several of the slobbering animals in her keep throw themselves wildly at the heavy-duty chain-link fence behind her. Cut to a shot of the partition between two gardens. Cut to Mr and Mrs Swain walking arm-in-arm, united in grief, along the pavement. Cut to the house of Tony Oxley, dog owner, with a fleeting glimpse of Mr Oxley himself behind a twitching curtain. The final on-location scene is a shot of two men manhandling the body of the dog, Casper, wrapped in a bin-liner, into an old van.

In a sequel to the episode, an interview takes place with Terry Singh, Bradford's long-serving dog warden, standing in front of his canary-yellow Black Maria in the fading Yorkshire twilight. Mr Singh says the usual things about responsible ownership, as he has done many times before during long summers when dog gangs go marauding through the streets of Bradford. Then he drives off into the night.

Your friend Noah says he used to work with Terry Singh, and he's a nice bloke. He also offers further evidence of the oscillating universe theory, based on the regular bursting of the water main outside his house, always during public holidays. The first time he noticed this occurrence was as he was walking home from the village one afternoon, and started to follow a stream of water flowing past him down the hill. Wondering about the source of the deluge, he battled against the tide for a quarter of a mile, and found himself standing in his own backyard, watching bubbling water forcing itself up through the surface.

This isn't a once-only event. Each time the pipe splits, thousands of gallons pour down the gravel driveway and out on to the road, forming something similar to the Ganges delta near the junction at the bottom, until men in blue boiler suits turn up two weeks later to staunch the flow.

This year the burst has been particularly annoying, given the so-called drought here in the county and the threat of rationing. Everyone around here knows how much it rains, but nevertheless, the newly privatized Yorkshire Water have somehow managed to spill most of it *en route* from the clouds to the taps, and official sources say it will now have to precipitate until the 12th of Never before ground-water levels are restored. Noah thinks that the water has been sold to Kuwait or Saudi Arabia, but apparently even countries with the hottest climates known to humankind have no need to buy, beg or borrow from elsewhere.

To overcome the drought problem, Yorkshire Water have initiated a military-style tankering operation, commissioning thousands of lorries to transport millions of gallons of the see-through stuff from a bottomless well at the far end of the county to a place at the top of the hill.

One night, you walk over the moor to take a look, following the glare of the arc lights and the noise of diesel engines, and the site from half a mile away looks like something from the Gulf War or Glastonbury Festival. Hundreds of vehicles are queuing up along the narrow road with their engines running, waiting to turn into the makeshift depot. Every cab has a different configuration of lights, including some with Christmas-tree lamps around the windscreen, and every driver has his elbow out of the open window. Men in luminous overalls run around outside with pipes and funnels and spanners and pieces of metal. Other men in suits and ties and duffle-coats and hard hats stroll though the complex with clipboards, pointing at things with their pens. The tankers that have emptied their contents slew around in the mud and turn back out on to the road, heading for the M62. You watch for about an hour and a half, unnoticed, then slosh back over the soggy moor for a bath.

Get them while they're hot, is the latest advice on the bath front, because according to this morning's *Yorkshire Post*, they could well be a thing of the past. According to rumours, YW have been considering the blanket banning of baths during the drought, as well as a suggestion that new houses should be built with shower-only bathrooms. At this week's inquiry into the water shortage, Yorkshire Water supremo Trevor Newton faced a 'six-hour lambasting', including allegations of mismanagement and basic stupidity. It's been a long hot summer for Mr Newton, a man in a permanent state of nervous sweating, it appears, and a man who seems determined to comb his hair into the shape and style of a wig. Earlier this year, after pledging allegiance to the cause and stating publicly that he'd given up his ablutions, he was caught nipping over the border to his sister's house for a jacuzzi, or so the story goes. Mr Newton, who takes early retirement in May, conceded during the debate that the drought had been a disaster, and at one point held out an empty glass, saying 'Chairman, if I may, I have just run out of water.' Mr Peter Bowler from Yorkshire Water Watch then offered him his own jug for £50. The inquiry continues, as does the gurgle of water from Noah's burst main, sluicing tons of gravel and cinders along the gutter towards the drain by the roundabout, as does the calculation of Yorkshire Water's pre-tax profits, to be announced at the end of the financial year.

The Tyre

One touch of nature makes the whole world kin,
That all with one consent praise new-born gawds,
Though they are made and moulded of things past – Shakespeare,
Troilus and Cressida

The human heart is like Indian rubber – Anne Brontë, *Agnes Grey*

Lo, all our pomp of yesterday
Is one with Nineveh and Tyre – Kipling, *Recessional*

You've just finished writing a poem about a tyre. In the first half
of the poem, you remember finding a tractor tyre on the moor
behind your parents' house, then rolling it down into the village
with four or five friends, to burn on Bonfire Night. Somewhere
during the last year or so, you've begun to think of your upbringing
as supernatural in some way, a notion based mainly on experiences
like this one with the tyre, experiences involving some element of
exploration or expedition, and quite often ending in mystery or
alchemy. In a similar incident, you and your friends made lead
ingots by melting down metal stripped from rooftops and windows,
having discovered all the necessary tackle buried in the earth under
the mill. Who'd left it there?

It wasn't unusual to go wandering off over the hills, just as it
wasn't unusual to find things in the middle of nowhere without
any reasonable explanation. A bag of golf balls on one occasion,
a pram, the bottom half of a turquoise bikini, and so on. In the
case of the tyre, we must have tripped right over it, because it was

sewn to the earth with tuft-grass and rushes, and the stitching had to be unpicked before we could prize it out of the peat and lift it up.

Growing up plays tricks with the brain, especially where weights and measures are concerned, and if in the end the tyre was actually the spare wheel from a Morris Minor, then so be it. But at the time it was massive; thick-skinned, hardly manageable, a huge monster of a thing, staggering blind drunk across the moor as we rolled it, using the diagonal wedges of its tread as handles.

You're more or less certain that the past, as some poets have already said, is a writer's only reserve. Almost all poems are the products of memory and recollection, as if the process of writing were an effort to recombine with that semi-conscious, half-innocent state of childhood, as if all poems were statements of loss. It's the same lamenting over the past that leads to so much anthropomorphism in poetry, and the sampling of inanimate objects for their human impressions to return to that dream-like country of 'before'. Having come too far to go back, we appeal to the super-conscious to win out over the everyday and the commonplace, to bring about some momentary flash of reconnection. Words are the conductors.

You're also thinking here about the way that very small children don't distinguish between the natural and the unnatural, the way that if a toy train chugged across the carpet under its own steam in front of a child, the laws of the universe wouldn't suddenly come into question. Once you were babysitting for a neighbour, and their little boy wouldn't go to sleep, and you could hear him fidgeting and grunting through the home-made intercom between the bedroom and downstairs. After a couple of hours, you flicked the switch on the tannoy and said, 'Go to sleep,' then flicked back in time to hear him saying to the loudspeaker, 'You shut up, Mr Box.' Animals have the same capabilities. Most people interpret this as the inability to determine between fact and fiction, as we grown-ups understand it.

In the second part of the poem, you describe what happened when the tyre reached the road. The village is down in the bottom of a geographical bowl, with all roads descending into it at a steep angle. This particular road is steeper than most, and straighter, and there came a point at which the tyre gained an unstoppable and terrible momentum. However much we tried to slow it down or tried to wobble it to the ground with rugby tackles and Kung-Fu kicks, it didn't even flinch, and carried on picking up speed towards the junction with the main road across the Pennines. At one stage, it even mounted the banking to turn a right-hand bend, then crossed the A62 between two wagons going at sixty miles an hour in opposite directions. You sometimes wonder if the two drivers ever jump from their sleep as a hundredweight of black rubber passes in front of the windscreen.

After the junction, the tyre careered on into the centre of the village, and we lost sight of it as it followed the camber of the street and turned to the left by the graveyard. Out of breath, with our hearts in our mouths and our hands black with the evidence, we entered the world of houses and shops, expecting broken glass and buckled metal at least, or at worst, the swatted fly of an upturned pram, with its wheels spinning in mid-air. But the tyre was nowhere. The giant vulcanized beast we'd brought to life had completely vanished; no one knew a thing about it, and being thankful and exhausted and children, we simply accepted it as a fact, and got on with the next thing.

There's probably more going on for you in the poem than there is for anyone who reads it. Your dad once made his living buying and selling tyres, so for you, those circles of carved rubber are a kind of currency or coinage. We'd be driving along some out-of-the-way road in North Yorkshire going across to the coast or up to Scotland on holiday, when he'd spy a haystack from a couple of fields away, with a sheet of black plastic over the top and half a dozen tyres holding it down. Ten minutes later you'd be sharing the back of the van with four remoulds and a pair of cross-plys, usually with water sloshing around inside them, and giving off heat like bread from the oven. Usually he'd pay for them, but there wasn't always anybody around to agree a price, so the tyres would jostle for room for the rest of the journey under an old oilcloth, like stolen sheep.

The only other time you saw your father take something that didn't belong to him was again on holiday, in Scotland, when he stopped the van at the side of a plantation of young pines, and asked your mother how much Christmas trees were going for these days. It was the middle of a very hot summer. We kept watch both ways while he pulled and wrestled with the little tree for what seemed like an hour, until the thing rocketed out of the earth and sent him spinning off into the woods. He came back covered in tiny cuts, with pine needles glued with sweat to his arms and face, and passed the mangled tree into the back of the van, still hung with a great clump of Scottish soil. When we were stopped for speeding in the Borders, you had to hold it down like a kidnapped child, and back at home he planted it in the bottom garden, away from the road, well out of sight. Pine trees mustn't travel well, or the soil wasn't right, or the shock of being attacked by your dad had finished it off. Within two weeks it was nothing but a skeleton, naked and shivering, and the rose-bay willow-herbs blew little fluffy white kisses at it from across the fence. Come Christmas, and maybe to make up for the failure, he came home with a tree that was so big it wouldn't come in through the door. Always someone to use the wrong tool if it was nearer than the right one, he went outside with a bread knife, but came back with the bottom half of the tree, having thrown the top part into the river. That year we had the only flat-topped Christmas tree in Christendom.

During the time when he was in the tyre trade, you hadn't realized how tight money must have been, until one week during the school holidays when you travelled around in the van with him. It was a bottle-green Ford Transit, with a double seat on the front passenger side, and something called a 'tickle-box' in the middle of the cabin, next to the driver's seat. What you remember about the tickle-box was that it made do as an extra seat in an emergency, and that it got very hot, especially for anyone wearing shorts who happened to brush against it with a bare leg. Its only use, as far as you could make out, was for keeping fish and chips warm on the way home. Vans don't have tickle-boxes any more – you've noticed this every time you've hired one to move house – or if they do, they've put them in the engine with all the other hot bits.

We drove around West Yorkshire for four days: Queensbury, Brighouse, Wakefield, Elland, stopping at garages and farms and mills and depots, but on Thursday night we still hadn't bought or sold a single tyre. On Friday we went further afield, places you'd never heard of and didn't recognize, out of his patch, and during the afternoon he talked less and less, and turned the radio off, and leant forward so he was almost driving with his chin on the steering wheel. Every time he stopped somewhere you'd wait in the van, watch him through the wing-mirror talking to men in brown boiler suits who were either shrugging their shoulders or shaking their heads. These silent conversations always ended with directions to another place we might try, or with a map drawn in the dust on the side of the van.

The light was going and he'd just about given up. We were driving back towards the motorway on the outskirts of Bradford, when he suddenly swung round in the middle of the road and pulled up at the top of a dirt-track running down to a dilapidated mill. He seemed to study the place for a couple of minutes, with the engine ticking over quietly, then dropped the handbrake and went bumping down the track towards the building. The inevitable Alsatian came tearing out of a half-eaten kennel, and was yanked back by a length of heavy-duty chain. Dad got out of the van and disappeared into the mill through a rolled-up metal door, and you sat there for twenty minutes, wondering how long you should wait before going inside to look for him. Suddenly he came jogging back out with a different look on his face, and drove the van around the rear of the building, into a courtyard where a man was wheeling a huge tractor tyre out of a garage, followed by another, then another, then another, until there were eight of the things leant against an old diesel tank. You hopped out and helped roll them up into the van, using two oily planks for a ramp. Before leaving, you watched him put his hand in his pocket, but the man waved him away, and half an hour later we were back at the garage in Huddersfield, with three filthy mechanics hauling the tyres out into the light, and your father doing business in the tatty little office with the blow-up Michelin Man beaming through the window. You don't know how much he got for them, but when we arrived home and he put the money in your mother's hand and folded her fingers across the wad of torn and dirty one-pound notes, she cried, and everything was good.

Maybe if he hadn't done the U-turn in the van and gone bouncing down that cinder-track, there wouldn't have been any money in the house that weekend. Maybe when he put his hand in his pocket back at the mill, there was nothing in it. Whatever the truth, he'd come home with a fortune, and after the tears had stopped we sat down in the living-room and started laughing hysterically at things that weren't even funny. It was the same day that a pole-cat had jumped out at your mother from behind the washer, so emotions were running pretty high.

The tyres were sold to exotic-sounding companies such as Honduras and Vacu-Lug, in exotic places such as Dewsbury and Keighley, to be remoulded. If they were too knackered, they went abroad, to Russia and East Germany. The remaining tread was ground off, manually, leaving a tyre 'carcass' on to which new raw-rubber treads were glued, the resin being sealed by heat in an oven as the tyre was 'cooked'. One of the reasons lorries are restricted to lower speeds is to stop a tyre becoming hot and shedding its skin. One of the reasons the hard-shoulders and central reservations of Britain's motorways are full of sloughed black hide is because wagons don't stick to the speed limit.

Tyres that were totally kaput went off to power stations to be 'crumbed' and burnt. Modern tyres won't break down in the same way because they're steel-braced, so have to be dumped in pot-holes and canyons, and burn for evermore if they catch fire, or become ecosystems for rodents and reptiles and certain plants if they don't. Dad still has theories about what to do with the world's unwanted tyres, including a plan to make a rubber path across the Pennine Way and other moorland walks, thus cutting down erosion, preventing the need to quarry expensive stone, and presumably solving the unemployment problem in the same stroke. He once went to Fort Dunlop, the Mecca of the tyre trade, on a three-week training course, and remembers that the factory was so big it had traffic lights inside the building. He also talks about one of the compounds in the tyre-making process as if it were a secret potion. Carbon Black. One teaspoon of this in its powder form, sneezed accidentally into a front-room, would coat every wall and every object in a shiny, black layer, indelibly. Those who worked in the business couldn't wash it off. It got into their skin, and under it.

When the company he worked for realized he was doing all right, they took the van off him, so he changed jobs and bought a Morris

Traveller. The Morris Traveller – the only car with timbers instead of welds. When it broke down, it was better to phone for a carpenter than a mechanic. After the Morris Traveller came the Morris Minor, which eventually suffered from the same problem as every other car of its kind. One night, Christmas Day probably, we were driving home from someone else's house, the car loaded up with presents, Dad taking it slowly down the steep hill into Crimble Clough, when suddenly a car wheel went past us on the outside and rounded the bend up ahead. We watched it for five or ten mesmerizing seconds, before realizing it was the small runaway wheel of a Morris Minor, and at the moment it dawned on us, the car tipped over on to the front axle on the offside, and we came to a slow, semi-circular halt in a shower of orange sparks. Dad walked down the hill into the darkness as if he was on the trail of the tyre, tracking it down, but half an hour later he came back in a fire engine, driven by a fireman he used to work with. We went home in the cab with the big horizontal steering-wheel and the cinemascope windscreen, leaving the Morris Minor with its nose to the ground like a dog asleep on a rug, and the tyre still rolling down the valley, over the bridge and out of the universe.

You inherited a succession of your father's cars. The Austin Princess with its leatherette seats that performed skin surgery on bare flesh in hot weather. The two-litre Datsun automatic that rode up at the front when you hit the accelerator, like a speedboat. Your mother borrowed it once but couldn't find the knob to turn the cassette player down, and drove her Mothers' Union friends to a meeting in town with The Fall's *Hex Enduction Hour* in wrap-a-round stereo at full tilt on looped playback. An amber-coloured Lada, oblong like a butterscotch, that boiled over every night on the ride back from Manchester, and needed water from the horse-trough at Globe Farm before coming home through the cutting. Another Lada that made a terrifying and expensive noise when you changed gear, like stirring a bag of glass with a metal poker.

Every vehicle carried the immovable smell of pipe tobacco, no matter how many forest-fresh plastic pennants you hung on the rear-view mirror. St Bruno ready-rubbed seemed to be growing down the back of every seat and in the carpet under the rubber mats. A sack of old, rusty tools was handed down with every car, like a bag of bones.

When you left the Probation Service and cashed in your chips and counted your savings, you had just about enough for a new car. A brand new car. This was in the days when car salesmen were hanging themselves on toilet chains at the back of garages because business was so bad; if you said 'no' for long enough, they'd throw in metallic paint, a sun-roof and seven years' membership of the RAC, not to mention the number-plate and a full tank of petrol.

Part of the ritual of buying a new car is to turn up at midnight on the last day of July and drive it home through the early hours of August with all the other arseholes in their new toys. Part of the ethos of buying a new VW is to enjoy it, because if the advertising is to be believed, you'll never need to do it again. This particular year, July 31st fell on a Friday, which meant that most of the customers collecting their new Passats and Golfs and Polos and Cabriolets were half-cut in the first place, and the dealership had laid on champagne and Buck's Fizz, plus soft drinks and cheese footballs as a sop to anyone who wanted to stay on the right side of the law.

The showroom was hung with banners and streamers, and for the fifteen minutes before the appointed time, the salesmen slimed their way around the crowd, congratulating the new owners, handing over key fobs and registration documents, and raising the possibility of an extended-warranty option. You sat in one of the show cars with the doors and windows closed and the radio on.

At midnight, after a final countdown and the release of hundreds of balloons from an old football net on the ceiling, the managing director of the franchise strolled out on to the balcony, took the microphone in his hand and said, 'Gentlemen, you may now go to your cars.'

It was the stuff of ceremony and sacrament, a future festival of ancient religion, the holiest day in the motorist's calendar. Bodies flooded across the forecourt, headlights blinked open and engines cleared their throats, and a convoy of L-registered Volkswagens – the people's car – turned right on to the ring road, into the witching hour.

Sport in the Region

Ian Rush, the man with the golden boot, has signed for Leeds United after a free transfer from Liverpool. In front of the *Look North* cameras, Howard Wilkinson unravels a tatty United scarf that looks more like an old beer towel, and holds it in front of an embarrassed-looking Rush, trying his hardest to conjure up a smile. Wilkinson looks uncomfortable as well, like a man who'd prefer to be dressed as Father Christmas, giving presents away in the children's ward at Leeds General, than pretending to be the manager of a Premier League football club. Pictures from earlier in the day show Rush in a sports jacket and red tie at a news conference, pledging his allegiance to his new club and looking forward to next season. The fact that he's now thirty-four and no longer of any use on Merseyside doesn't seem to be bothering anyone, least of all Howard Wilkinson, and Rush tells the camera how hungry he is for goals and how he never settles for second best. Rush in a white shirt might be a difficult thing to imagine, but it's his Liverpudlianism that's more troubling than anything else, being so blatantly and unapologetically a Scouser that he must be some kind of Trojan horse, sent across the Pennines to damage Yorkshire football from the inside. Even if he did manage to score fifty goals with Tony Yeboah next year, it would be an act of charity.

They spare Rush the humiliation of pulling on the United strip and juggling footballs in the rain, and instead we watch footage

57

of him scoring three or four goals for Liverpool from an era when shorts were not the knee-length bloomers they are today but skin-tight satin knickers. The final shot of the programme shows Rush and Wilkinson together again, joined by the scarf, almost with their arms around each other but not quite, with Rush smiling through clenched teeth and Wilkinson staring beyond the camera into the middle distance. It's been a strange year for Howard, downhill most of the way since the signing of Tomas Brolin, football's answer to Elmer Fudd, who spent most of the season playing with the zip on his tracksuit. Wilkinson's been accused of not being interested any more, and even now he has the look of a man dreaming of home, a quiet night in with the family, sitting down in front of the telly with his tea on a tray and the dog at his feet with his slippers in its mouth.

David Seaman is a national hero after snuffing out the Spanish attack in the quarter-finals of the European Championship and parrying Nadal's spot-kick round the post in the penalty shoot-out. *Calendar* have gone along to Rotherham, Seaman's home town, to sample local pride in the big man's achievements, and over pints of bitter in a working men's club, under the dartboard, some early-evening drinkers offer their expert opinions. 'Top bloke, he is,' says one man from behind his glass. 'Top player.' Somewhere in the background another voice says, 'David Seaman. He's a goalkeeper.' No one recalls Seaman's previous performance against a Spanish side, back-pedalling like a man falling off a step-ladder as Nayim's fifty-yard nine-iron plopped into the net behind him. No one mentions the haircut, the police moustache.

In the cricket, Yorkshire are top of the County Championship for the first time in living memory, despite going for 681 against Leicestershire last Thursday, the most runs conceded by Yorkshire in an innings since . . . the last time. Most afternoons, you call at your father's to watch county cricket the way most other people watch it these days – on Ceefax. Between the updates, he flicks through the teletext pages, trying his luck with the quizzes and checking the peseta against the pound for this summer's holiday. We go into the garden and he taps out his pipe on the patio steps and trails the watering can along a row of yellow roses. He's built a pergola over the garden path out of heavy timber – flying buttresses shackled together with steel brackets – and he thumps it with the outside of his fist to test its strength. It looks like the framework for a Spanish man-of-war or a cathedral roof, and sweet-peas are beginning to twist around its footings, spiralling upwards. We go back inside to see Yorkshire's overseas player Michael Bevan cruise to yet another fifty, and speculate as to why the rest of the team can't manage it. Bevan's probably the best batsman in England at the moment and can't even get in the Australian test side, but as long as he's scoring runs for us, we don't care if he's from the planet Mars. And as Ray Illingworth says, 'When Yorkshire are strong, England are strong,' although this maxim must have been coined at a time when the best players in the county were actually eligible to play for their country.

England, as it happens, are one-nil up against India, and batting out for a draw in the second test at Lord's. In an uneventful game, the most notable feature of the contest has been Dickie Bird's retirement from test umpiring. Five days ago he fought his way through the orange and yellow ties of the upstanding members of the MCC and walked to the middle, dabbing at the tears behind his glasses. It's no secret that Mr Bird is a man who exists in very close proximity to his emotions, a characteristic first revealed on *This Is Your Life*, when he greeted every Freeman, Hardy and Willis who walked on to stage as a twin brother, separated at birth.

All Points North

At the end of his final test match, umpire Harold Bird is led from the field by half a dozen shirt-sleeved policemen like a runaway boy after a lifetime's adventure.

Poetry versus the Rest of the World

You've been asked to keep wicket in the *TLS* cricket match. Poetry v. Prose. You phone Mick Imlah, the organizer, and leave a message that you know another writer who happens to be a very quick bowler and not a bad batsman, if we're short. A couple of days later he phones back. 'This writer. It isn't Margaret Drabble, is it?'

The last time you played cricket with Mick was in Japan, on a British Council reading trip, billed as *The Wingèd Muse* tour. Every night after drinks, the team netted for a couple of hours along the wooden passageway of the house they were staying in, using a squash ball and an umbrella. Most of the walls in the house were made out of paper, and after a fortnight it looked like a meteorite shower had passed through it.

You meet Glyn Maxwell on the way to the ground, and start fantasizing about the team. Heaney coming in at number six and smiting a quick fifty before holing out at long-on. Hughes taking four for thirty-six bowling his leg-breaks up hill into the rough. Carol Ann Duffy and Wendy Cope buttering the bread for the sandwiches in the tiny kitchen at the back of the pavilion. Maybe not.

In the event, the warm-up tour of the Far East pays dividends, with Armitage and Imlah undefeated at the wicket with a hundred and twenty odd between them, most of Armitage's runs being baseball-batted through mid-off or heaved over square leg into the trees on the short boundary. A hawk hovers over the ground all afternoon, sometimes folding and falling into the long grass above the railway line, then rising again and treading the air above the goings-on at the wicket, like a new version of the third umpire. At the end of the evening, the poets are popping champagne corks on the balcony and showering a delirious, capacity crowd with froth and bubbles. A threadbare flag flies at half-mast over Shepherd's Bush Cricket Club, signifying the death of the novel.

North Riding

With nothing much happening at the moment, and the bowling fixtures cancelled during the Huddersfield Textile holidays, you drive up to North Yorkshire. You pull up in the car park in Helmsley, next to the enormous new toilet-block built in the same style and stone as Sainsbury's supermarkets, and walk through the woods and fields to Rievaulx. In the Ionic Temple on the terrace above the ancient abbey, a couple from Dewsbury are talking to the National Trust curator about bus timetables and concessional rates for pensioners.

'We can go anywhere we want now, for a pound, can't we, Frank?' says the woman.

'I'm sure you can,' says the curator. 'Have you noticed this central fresco? It's been restored after one of the workmen put his foot through the ceiling.'

'Has it really? Because we'd never heard of this place till somebody told us, and we've come up today on the bus and it's only cost us a pound, hasn't it, Frank?'

'Well, now you've found us, I hope you'll visit us again.'

'No, we shan't,' says the woman, 'because we've seen it now.'

Ten minutes later, Frank trips over a poodle tethered to a foot-scraper at the top of the steps, and arrives head-first into the exhibition in the basement, followed closely by his wife, cursing all dogs and their owners. 'Come here,' she says, 'you've muckied your trousers.' She bends over him, inspecting the dirty mark on his knee and spitting on to a handkerchief.

You drive across to the coast to Robin Hood's Bay for the night, and after fish and chips on the beach attended by a squadron of dive-bombing seagulls, get involved in a pub quiz in the Laurel Inn, and finish with the disappointing score of nine out of twenty-five. You leave by the side door when an argument breaks out over the colour of Noddy's hat.

At the top of the hill you watch the yellow-orange of Jupiter, low down in the south-west, and work out a way of measuring the distance of the moon from the earth using two pieces of string, two conkers, a protractor and a good watch. The fact that the Egyptians thought of it three thousand years ago doesn't stop you congratulating yourself on your moment of astronomical brilliance.

Next day, you walk to the Raven Hotel on the cliff-tops at Ravenscar, home to the Bulgarian football team during the European Championships last month, who checked out halfway through the tournament because of the lack of 'action' in and around the establishment. After waiting an hour and a half for a cheese roll and a slice of malt-loaf, you're in complete sympathy with them, and wander back along a disused railway line. Looking at the hotel from a distance, it's an impressive sight, and has the added advantage of still being about a hundred yards from the North Sea, which is munching its way inland at an alarming rate of knots these days. A few years ago, a man in a hotel in Scarborough looked out of his bedroom window, and found the sea view he'd requested to be almost *en suite*. A week later, the gardens and building slipped into the waves, with residents standing around at the top of the drive complaining that they'd been asked to settle their bills before leaving.

On the following morning, you go and watch Yorkshire getting hammered by Somerset at Scarborough, then drive back across the moors, finding yourself at Helmsley toilets again before turning south for Leeds. Inside the building, above the taps, there's a notice saying PLEASE DO NOT WASH FOOTWEAR IN THESE SINKS, signed by the Chief Technical Officer of Ryedale District Council, and above the hand-dryer there's a plaque commemorating the *1989 Loo of the Year Award*, presented to Helmsley car park. To add to its achievement, customers have written their own comments on scraps of paper or business cards and dropped them down inside the glass frame. One reads, 'Best of British Bogs – not all eating places are as clean (Cumbria),' and another, 'I thought they smelt a bit, but I'll come again, they're lovely. Steve.' Someone else has drawn a man with a long nose peering over a wall, and written underneath it, 'Wat, no rubbers?' It's a flash-back to the McCondom machine in the toilets at the Laurel Inn, vending packets of three, each flavoured with a single malt and containing the warning, 'This product should not be used while driving.'

Man About Town

Huddersfield. You drive to the next village to pick up a letter from the post-office depot. Someone's written and not put a stamp on the envelope. It's warm, but wet with a fine drizzle. In the forecourt of the warehouse next door, five men in blue boiler suits are playing cricket in their dinner hour, using a child's cricket bat and an upturned oil drum for the stumps. A West Indian at the wicket looks like he's digging in for a long innings, and cover-drives the shaggy tennis ball towards you, between two parked cars. You field it with your right hand and shy at the oil drum, but miss. The ball splatters against a spotless new BMW, leaving a big brown stain next to the petrol cap. All the fielders cheer, and one of them shouts, 'It's the gaffer's.' At just about every bus-stop on the way into town there's a woman in a Sainsbury's uniform, unmistakable with the quilted blue jacket and orange trim, the orange blouse and the blue knee-length skirt. The new Land Army.

At the travel agent's, you're trying to book a complicated flight to Richmond in Virginia, then back from Boston, but end up ear-wigging the conversation at the next desk. A young couple with a screaming toddler are asking about vacancies at Pontin's or Butlin's, and the man behind the counter, tapping away at a computer, has finally come up with something at Prestatyn Sands. 'There's a value room or a standard room. The value rooms are the basic, and the standards are a bit more modern.'

'What's the price?' asks the woman.

'£166 for the standard, £144 for the value.'

'Oh, we'd better have the value,' she says, and her husband nods his head, agreeing with her.

You feel like passing her the twenty-two quid, but wouldn't dream of showing her up, and even the travel agent looks like he's thinking the same thing. 'Let's see if they'll do anything better, for the money,' he says, and picks up the phone.

Meanwhile, you're getting nowhere with Anthea, your 'Flight Consultant', who only seems able to find flights that depart from inaccessible English suburbs in the small hours of the morning and arrive in dangerous American cities during hours of darkness. At one stage she telephones through to another airline, and begins by telling the person at the other end who she is and where she's phoning from.

'Huddersfield,' she says.

Pause.

'Huddersfield.'

Pause.

'H-U-D-D-E-R-S-F-I-E-L-D. Haven't you heard of it?'

Pause.

'No, actually. It's very nice.'

You leave the shop clutching a reference number for a provisional booking you know you won't use, too embarrassed to go on discussing the price of an open-jaw ticket to the New World when the next couple are emptying their pockets on to the table and scrabbling for pound coins in the bottom of a shopping bag.

In the precinct, you see a kid you went to school with, wearing a Huddersfield Town shirt and selling balloons, although you don't suppose he is a kid any longer, he's a man. He has a beard and a tattoo of a Yorkshire terrier on his forearm. As you get near to him, you can't remember who is supposed to look away, you or him, but in the event you both turn your heads and pretend not to have seen each other. In Sainsbury's, you're paying for a pint of milk and a loaf of bread with a credit card and staring down the line of checkouts – like a starting trap at a dog track. Suddenly the cashier's waving a receipt, two ten-pound notes and a cash-back slip under your nose, asking you to write on the back of the slip, 'to say that you've had it'. You're miles away, and it's only after you've written, 'I HAVE HAD IT,' and handed it over that you realize it was a signature she was after. You're both too flustered to put matters right, and back in the car you sit for five minutes, letting the fine rain drift in through the open window and cool the blood in your cheeks.

Sport in the Region

First visit of the season to the McAlpine Stadium to see Town against Southend. You did go last week with Craig to see them against West Brom, but when you got to within a hundred yards of the ground without seeing a single blue and white shirt or a hot-dog van, you realized they were playing away. This isn't the kind of support that the club need.

Even though the stadium has won several design awards, it still isn't finished, with one end of the ground being completely open, as if someone forgot to close the door. At full time it's nil–nil, with Town lucky, as they say, to have got nil. Walking back along St Andrew's Road you make the mistake of asking the only autistic boy at the match if he's heard any other scores, and he follows you all the way back to the car with his transistor radio, tugging your sleeve and shouting out results from the Vauxhall Conference League.

On the Sunday you drive over to Craig's in Scissett to watch United v. Newcastle on Sky in his local pub. Allegiance to the bigger clubs is a village-to-village thing in these parts, and the Barnsley fans in the Crown are already cheering as we walk in to find Darren Peacock scoring an unlikely and suspicious goal on the big screen in the corner. You stay near the cigarette machine, and force a smile. Sometime during the first half, there's a flare-up between Nicky Butt and David Batty, an incident that definitely contains some element of east meets west, in a trans-Pennine sort of way. Butt is one of United's crop of home-grown wonder-kids, which makes him a Lancastrian, whether he was born in Manchester or anywhere else, and whether he likes it or not. He also has ginger hair. David Batty is very much a son of Leeds, and despite his moves to Blackburn and then Newcastle, you've never heard anyone around here say a wrong word about him. He's blond, and even though his hair is longer than it used to be, he's a skinhead. It's the tonsorial version of the War of the Roses.

Butt falls over in the tackle and kicks out at Batty, so Batty leaves a foot in as he strides over him. Butt stands up and jabs Batty in the chest two or three times with his fingers, at which Batty leans forward and takes Butt by the throat, with one hand. End of argument. The reaction in the pub isn't a cheer or even one of those howler monkey noises made at boxing matches, but laughter, and lots of it.

Final score: a double victory for the Barnsley fans; five United players get booked – one for every goal they let in.

Where There's Muck

To the Lawrence Batley Theatre in Huddersfield to see *Hamlet*. Lawrence Batley is a local supermarket tycoon who also has one of the stands at the McAlpine Stadium named after him. It's troubling that a person can buy this kind of civic respectability rather than earn it or have it bestowed on him by the powers that be, although for all you know, Lawrence Batley might be the most wonderful man in the world. And it's probably his name that rankles more than anything else, or gives rise to certain suspicions you have about him. Lawrence Batley. It smacks of a northern upward mobility – that giveaway Yorkshire surname, with Lawrence to preface it as a kind of disclaimer, or something to separate him from the rest of the tribe.

Another groundless prejudice you have against him comes from working in a supermarket when you were sixteen, unloading slippery cartons of butter and margarine from delivery wagons into a stinking cellar under the shop. The shoes you wore went rancid, and on the day you left, two of the warehouse staff put you in the bailing-machine used for compressing cardboard boxes, and left it running till you screamed. You think of this experience as your contribution to the personal fortune of all northern supermarket tycoons, and always remember the huge, hydraulic vice closing in, James Bond style, whenever you're pushing through the turnstile at the ground or picking up tickets from the theatre box-office.

In fact, being trapped in a shrinking space is not unlike watching tonight's performance, except in this case the torture goes on for three hours and doesn't stop until every inch of life is squeezed out of it. The leading man, as the *Huddersfield Examiner* accurately points out next day, could never be Hamlet if he lived to be a million, and Gertrude is the woman from the Nescafé advert who looks like Helen Daniels out of *Neighbours*. She appears to have a wooden leg, or even a metal one. When she falls to the floor with a clank at the end of the play, the man behind me starts humming the theme tune.

You're with Noah and his parents, which is interesting, because Noah's first-ever excursion into amateur dramatics ended in a similar way. In *Murder at Deam House*, he was shot in the back by a mystery assailant, and discovered in a pool of blood by the lady of the house having been woken by the sound of a gun. As she rolled him over and declared, 'He's dead,' the hundred-and-fifty-strong audience in Marsden Parochial Hall squealed with laughter, unconvinced by his departure from this world into the next. He's also remembered for having forgotten the very first line in his short career as a thespian, which was 'Hello,' and should have been delivered from the wings.

Noah's parents enjoy *Hamlet*, which is a relief after the hell they went through last time they came Up North. Noah had phoned up in the afternoon to say they were visiting and he didn't know what to do with them, so you suggested a film, and said you'd go with them for something to do. Noah looked through the listings to find something uncontroversial and inoffensive. There wasn't much on, apart from a film called *Paris Trout*, and even though he knew it wouldn't be about fly-fishing on the Left Bank, he thought it sounded pleasant enough and a good way of killing a couple of hours on a Saturday night with his parents in tow.

The first danger sign came in the title sequence, when the name Dennis Hopper flashed across the screen, and you saw Noah, three seats away, bring his hand to his forehead. True to form, about an hour into the story and just when things were going fairly smoothly, Mr Hopper took it upon himself to sexually assault his wife with what looked like a Coca-Cola bottle. As a scene, it probably lasted about a minute, but as an experience it took something in excess of a century to come to an end. On any occasion it would have felt ugly, cheap, unnecessary, but in those very particular circumstances it was nothing less than a nightmare. In the next seat, Noah's dad reached into his anorak for his pipe, and without lighting it began sucking furiously at the mouthpiece. In the seat next to him, Noah's mother wrapped and unwrapped a Nuttall's Mintoe several times, finally lifted it to her mouth but stopped short of her lips and popped it into the ashtray in front of her. In the seat next to her, Noah glared at the screen, like a hundred-metre runner in the blocks, his eyes fixed on the finishing line. When we all filed out of the back door of the cinema into Bradford's Little Germany, there was a long and very obvious silence, eventually broken by Noah's mother, who said, 'The wallpaper in that house . . . was just like some your Auntie Barbara used to have in her bathroom.' We walked back to the car, slowly, and a group of students overtook us, reviewing the film, sounding off knowledgeably about screen violence and product placement.

Lawrence Batley appears in the December issue of *Yorkshire Life*, but 'the eighty-five-year-old with an ego to match his fortune' will probably be disappointed not to have made it to the front cover. In fact, it's not until page forty-six that Mr Batley features in an article entitled *Entrepreneur Life*, under the heading '20th Century Victorian', explaining his life-long motto, 'The best is good enough for me.' Asked about his motives for wanting his 'name above the door', he replies, 'It's a massive boost for my ego, and if I said it didn't matter, I would be a hypocrite.' Personalized buildings make a change from number-plates, but of course he has one of those as well. He stands in front of his big swanky car, LB1, a tiny man in a golf shirt and matching socks. The top button of his fly might be undone. He rests his hand on the bonnet and his knee against the bumper. It's a demonstration of ownership and pride, but looks like he forgot to put the handbrake on.

The magazine also goes 'Behind the scenes at Harvey Nicks'. When the Knightsbridge store opened its new branch in Leeds, *Look North* went along to report, with the beautiful Sophie Rayworth coming live from the menswear section inside the crowded shop. On a large tangerine settee, a man from the firm's management with wide lapels and what your father always refers to as 'correspondent shoes' talked effortlessly about the demand for classic styles and designer goods in the prosperous North. The camera then swung to the person sat next to him, a nervous-looking individual perched on the edge of the sofa, obviously not one of HN's regular customers.

Your mother, who's videoed the programme, turns up the volume with the remote. It isn't clear if the character in the picture has anything to do with the proceedings, or if he's just been dragged in off the street to say something. With a red face, he mumbles something about a clash of images, about cloth caps and Lady Di's smalls, and then it's back to the studio for a round-up of the day's other news.

'Is that it?' your mum asks.

'Yep,' you say.

'Did they pay you?'

'Nope,' you say.

Silence.

'Well,' she says, 'it was very good.'

News Just In

A man from Halifax has failed in his attempt to earn a place in the *Guinness Book of Records*. After spending almost a month living in a tree in his friend's garden, he came down to earth only to find that the world record was not twenty-six days, as he had been told, but twenty-six years. The record was set by a man in Indonesia, who climbed a palm tree in the early seventies, and still hasn't come down.

Interviewed by the *Yorkshire Post*, Mr Chris Lee said, 'I feel a right prat.' The attempt was made in a two-hundred-and-fifty-year-old sycamore at an altitude of forty feet. Mr Lee hoisted up food in a bucket, slept in a sleeping bag wedged between branches, and took with him a supply of books to read, including the Yellow Pages.

Over the Top into Lancashire

Every other Monday night for the past three years, you've made the same drive over the top – across the Pennines, down to the end of the A62, through Manchester city centre and pulled up at the side gates of the BBC on Charles Street. After the obligatory twenty questions by the security guard in his little sentry box, he eventually gets bored and lets you in. You usually leave the car in a parking space with the words 'Head of Religion' written on the tarmac (thinking that anyone professionally religious should be in bed by this time), and run up the back stairs and along the corridor into Studio 5, for *The Mark Radcliffe Show*. Then between ten and midnight, on Radio 1, you read poetry: Chaucer, Keats, Virgil, Coleridge, Dickinson, Housman, Catullus, Hardy, Whitman, Hopkins, Frost, Yeats, Auden, Plath . . . anyone. Everyone. Somebody said to you once that those poets would turn in their graves if they heard their work being broadcast on the nation's pop-music network, but with a few exceptions you disagree. And there's even more pleasure to be had from reading work by living poets, those sitting down to supper in Radio 3 land, blissfully unaware that you're giving their work its biggest-ever audience on a neighbouring frequency.

You used to wonder if anyone was interested or even irritated by these outbursts of verse between Teenage Fanclub and Sparklehorse and Cud and Echo and the Bunnymen and Blur, but now you just think of it as all part of the same thing, and admire the people who run the show for letting you get on with it without the addition of jingles or back-beats – the radio equivalent of arm-bands or stabilizers. There's also a large element of self-indulgence, getting to meet the bands that featured on the soundtrack of *The Life and Times of Simon Armitage*, and going home with a handful of CDs.

Tonight, though, Mark's away on holiday, and you got a message last week to say that John Peel would be doing the show. You were sixteen or seventeen when you first heard him on the radio, when *The John Peel Show* was this very slot – ten till midnight, Monday to Thursday – and there probably hasn't been a day since then when you haven't played or whistled or finger-drummed or hummed or air-guitared or actually strummed along to some tune that he played before anyone else did. At school, you and your friend Rob used to take it in turns to record his show, edit the best bits, and swap tapes on the school bus. You always thought Peel knew you were doing this, and approved of it, because he never spoke a word until the last note of every record had dissolved into silence.

Not that it would have mattered if he had started to speak. His comments and quips and mumblings were just as important as the music, as were his technical hitches, which included playing at least two records per night at the wrong speed, and talking at great length about somebody's new single before playing the B-side. Such cock-ups usually ended in Peel apologizing through a burst of laughter as he dragged the needle across the vinyl and flipped the record over, or cranked the turntable up to the right speed. I still can't listen to the twelve-inch version of *Atmosphere* by Joy Division without anticipating the moment when Ian Curtis changes gear from 33⅓ to 45 r.p.m., about three seconds into the opening line.

Peel once said that people ask if they can come in to watch him do the show, but that there's nothing to see apart from a man in a room who looks to be sat at a typewriter. When you walk into the studio, about an hour before the programme, he's busy scribbling a letter and listening to something on the headphones, and doesn't notice you for about a minute. He probably looks older than when you've seen him in photographs or on the telly, but you've always admired the way he attracts the attention of younger generations without ever attempting or pretending to be part of them. He's pale as well, looks tired, and you've read in a magazine that his wife is ill. When he looks up, he pulls off the headphones and apologizes. He's in the middle of dubbing a bootleg cassette of Captain Beefheart at a legendary gig in Kidderminster, at which Peel was roadie, MC, and chauffeur by the sound of it. P. J. Harvey has asked him for a copy of the tape, and as he chats with the sound-recordist over the talk-back, you suddenly feel very satisfied and smug, not because you've finally met the man himself, but because he's every bit as . . . well, every bit as John Peel as you thought he was and wanted him to be. Most obvious is his interest in things other than himself, something that separates him from most of his colleagues, and probably saved him from the last clear-out, when half of his contemporaries were given the boot, and flounced out of Broadcasting House, taking their egos with them. His manner as well is something that sets him apart; most people use the words 'please' and 'thank you' either through gritted teeth or as if they were promotional gimmicks in a politeness-marketing strategy. But with him, you get the feeling he actually knows what they mean, and actually means them.

You sit down and start chatting about what you do on the show, and he apologizes again, for not knowing much about you, for not being any good at interviewing people on the radio, for not knowing which records are which, which buttons to press, and so on. He tells you how much he misses his family when he's away from home, including his son, William, who he describes as 'the slacker's slacker'. He says, 'His indolence is quite breathtaking. I think he must practise.' For some reason, we end up talking about swearing, and you tell him the old story about the poet reading in a school, being ticked off by the headmaster, who says to him, 'This school doesn't like poems with language in them.' He begins describing a similar experience on the air-waves, when he once DJ'd a live programme with John Lennon and Yoko from a studio in London. During the show, he had to read out a number of messages, and Lennon suggested that they all do it together, each of them reading one line of the announcement at a time. Lennon then suggested that they should punctuate the delivery with long, random pauses, which they did. The next day the BBC received a complaint from a vicar in the West Country, saying that the silences were 'obscene'. Telling me this, and after mentioning Lennon for the third time, he refers to him simply as 'John', then stops and rolls his eyes, embarrassed to be speaking about him in first-name terms. He says, 'John! Well, it was his name.'

Telling Rob about him in the pub the next night, about him, John Peel, John, you blush, and find yourself saying, 'Well, it's his name.'

The programme goes very well, despite him trying to play the reverse side of a CD at one stage, and the fact that you never get around to reading any of the poems you've taken along, just content to ramble on about everything and nothing, with him playing a record every time you run out of breath. Between the chat, you begin to wonder if there's some universal principle to be learned here, such as the fact that all living legends who are worth getting to know are neither impressed by their own fame, nor indifferent to it, but just slightly baffled. Leaving the studio and driving home, you listen to the last ten minutes of the show on the car radio, and hear him playing some slushy old love song not mentioned on the playlist, dedicating it to his wife.

Quiz Night Down at the Club

Question-master: What is a topee?
Contestant: A helmet.
Question-master: No, it's a wig.
Contestant: You mean a toupee.
Question-master: No, that's a wigwam.
Contestant: No, that's a tee-pee.
Question-master: Same difference.

Over the Top into Lancashire

Reading in the theatre at Oldham Sixth Form College. Beforehand, you're writing out a list of poems to read, a 'set list', and decide to begin with *The Winner*, a piece about a boy who loses all of his limbs and organs and digits, one at a time, and has them replaced with ridiculous mechanical contraptions. The boy goes on to receive a medal for swimming and a badge for completing a long walk, and the poem is about modest achievement in the face of torrential circumstances, plus the pathetic smile that goes with it. You got the idea for the poem when you were having problems with your blood and your bones, and used to wake up every morning with pins and needles or numbness, or various parts of your body still fast asleep. You were also thinking of a joke your dad used to tell about the British prisoner of war being held by the Germans, who has to have an arm amputated, and asks if the limb can be sent back to England to be buried. The same thing happens with his other arm, then his right leg, but when he has to have his left leg removed and makes the same request, the authorities say no. The commandant tells him, 'We think you're trying to escape.'

About five minutes before you're due to start, you notice a man come into the foyer to buy a ticket for the reading, who, as he bends his elbow, slides a shiny metal claw out from the bottom of his sleeve. You put a question mark next to the poem and go into the toilets. The next man to come in through the door is the man with the metal hand, who stands beside you and unzips his trousers. It's an unwritten rule of the gentlemen's urinal that eyes should face front at all times, unless of course you're on your own, in which case you're allowed to watch the inevitable cigarette butt floating to the end of the trough, or check to see if you're in proper working order. So when you walk on to the stage two minutes later, you've no idea how useful and sensitive the claw might be, or if the man has other engineered components about his person, like the boy in the poem. You look out into the audience and catch sight of him straight away, about halfway back in the middle. You see the poem in front of you. It's one of those situations where to go ahead and do it could be exactly right, or perfectly wrong. There's a long pause, and an ambulance goes past outside with its siren moaning.

The week after, at the Updates 'A' Level English conference on 11th November, you're giving a talk on revision and drafting in poetry to about two thousand students in the new Bridgewater Hall, in Manchester. The hall, built to replace the Free Trade Hall as the North's foremost classical-music venue, is constructed internally in glass, chrome, and light wood, and has the look and the feel of an ocean liner after a refit. It's also built on springs to absorb the rumble of traffic and trains from outside and underneath. If everyone jumps up and down at the same time, it can be pogoed along Deansgate into Victoria Station.

You finish speaking just before eleven o'clock, and announce the two-minute silence, introduced this year as the weekday version of Remembrance Sunday, for those people too busy at the weekend. Total quiet is always strange, but in one of the world's greatest acoustics, it's deafening – a great volume of nothing waiting for something to silence it by speaking out. And two minutes of private thought goes on eternally in a public space. It's a relief at the stroke of eleven itself when hundreds of digital watches start pipping and beeping and playing tunes, as if a cage of balloons or birds had been opened from the ceiling.

The Film Set

You're suspicious about film. For one thing, it's still a baby – less than a hundred years old, and only just at the potty-training stage in comparison with certain other ancient and well-practised art forms, poetry for instance. For another thing, it's a fairly passive medium, requiring very little of its audience short of not falling asleep. Film rests very comfortably on the retina, whereas printed words seem to get right down through the optic nerve, like microbes of thought, inflaming the imagination.

At best, films are made by collectives. At worst, they're made by companies, or rather by corporations, and what tends to get lost is that single strand of individual thought that we admire so much in, say, a novel. Which brings you to your real grumble. It's reckoned that about 80 per cent of all films are remakes of books, and therefore secondary in nature, and more often than not, inferior. This isn't universally the case, of course, but it seems that most films hang around books like thieves in a car park, trying the door handles of other people's vehicles.

As a rule, the greater the book, the poorer the film. This isn't just because the film tends to suffer by comparison, but because it comes a cropper in assuming the same artistic status as the original: it's Shakespeare, so it must be good. But far and away the worst flicks are those that dabble in poetry, with poetry 'cast' in the same way an actor is, usually in a serious or sensitive role. Recent culprits, among many, are the wretched *Dead Poets' Society* and the truly crummy *Tom and Viv*. Add to this most actors' apparent mission in life to murder poetry by performing it when it only need be said, and the picture is a bleak one. Even the rendition of Auden's 'Funeral Blues', recited during *Four Weddings and a Funeral*, was, to be honest, ordinary, but presumably received such unstoppable praise because of the lack of decent competition. Film of the book – ho hum. Film of a book about poets – shudder.

You're admitting to all these prejudices to let it be known that you're the wrong man for the job – the job being to attend the filming of the Pat Barker novel, *Regeneration*, a story based around the meeting of poets Siegfried Sassoon and Wilfred Owen at Craiglockhart Hospital at the time of their convalescence during the First World War. Sassoon had found his way to Craiglockhart via the interventions of Robert Graves, a fellow officer in the trenches, who saved Sassoon from a certain court martial following his public declaration against the war effort and the throwing of his Military Cross into the Mersey. Owen was recuperating after a fierce battle near St Quentin, and suffering from nerve damage and speech disruption – two classic symptoms of trench warfare. The book's other major character is W. H. R. Rivers, the Freudian psychologist trying to coax shell-shocked servicemen out of their neurasthenia and back into the land of the living. Rivers is played by Jonathan Pryce, recently returned from sharing a balcony with Madonna in the film-musical *Evita*, and lining up alongside him in less presidential circumstances are James Wilby as Sassoon, and Stuart Bunce as Owen. The film also boasts the addition of 'Trainspotter' Jonny Lee Miller as Prior, a fictional character, whose love-interest with Sarah (Canadian actress Tanya Allen) provides a sensual and excruciating parallel with Dr Rivers' unspoken feelings towards a sympathetic but unreciprocating 2nd Lieutenant Sassoon.

Most of the filming has been done in and around Glasgow, and on the way up, you read through Allan Scott's script, which is excellent – much of the dialogue lifted straight from Barker's novel – and captures perfectly the struggle between bearing up and breaking down that characterized the predicament of the officer classes during the later stages of the Great War. Owen's stuttering shyness, Rivers' clipped, professional English, and Sassoon's reserve as an officer and a gentleman are measured and weighed against agonizing monologues of nerve-torn gibberish fulled by rage, humiliation and fear. In and amongst, lines of poetry float past like subtitles – detached, conclusive.

The taxi driver doesn't think this is the right part of town for a film set, and still thinks you're a lunatic when he drops you off in the covered yard of what looks like an old coach-works with derelict warehousing on three sides. So much for the glamour of the film world; it's just above freezing, but only just, and rain dribbles in through holes in the roof. You're taken up a rickety metal fire-escape and whisked round the production offices – temporary rooms partitioned with fibreboard and sloshed with white paint, like the headquarters of some illegitimate business, here one day, gone the next. There's a sign on the toilet door saying, 'Gentlemen, we realize that construction work is messy, but there is no excuse for dropping toilet paper on the floor.' Underneath, somebody at the construction end of things has written, 'Bollox.'

'This is Simon Armitage – he's a poet,' someone explains as she tours you from one room to the next, and it's at this point that you begin to wonder why you've been flown up to Scotland for the day. Is it really for a quick look at the film set of the-next-big-British-film, or are you supposed to provide some talismanic presence, a kind of poet's blessing of the project during these last days of filming? Either way, everyone's extremely welcoming, and all the smiling faces looking up from their computer screens and editing desks tell the story of a good thing coming to a successful conclusion. Everyone looks very, very chuffed.

You're always impressed by the number of people to be thanked and credited at the end of a feature film, but hadn't anticipated that everyone involved in *Regeneration* would need to be on location at the same time, from some of the film's financial backers to the best boy's third apprentice, making the set like a community of ants or a beehive. Somewhere in the middle is a central chamber. Around it, a legion of caddies and flunkies and gophers, all in regulation puffa jackets and Timberland boots, all clomping about with clipboards and walkie-talkies and rolls of gaffer-tape around their wrists. A bell rings in the yard and everyone stops dead in their tracks, like musical statues. The bell sounds twice, and every-one starts running around again. At least, that's how it looks from the top of the fire-escape, and eventually (after two rings on the bell) you're escorted to the ground floor and through a heavy, grease-stained curtain, to get a slice of the action.

The Wilfred Owen Society were not impressed, apparently, when it was announced that the actual Craiglockhart Hospital in Edin-burgh – still up and running – would not be used for filming for practical reasons. Instead, its atmosphere and interiors would be recreated in a dilapidated industrial shed in Glasgow. At first sight, the artificial Craiglockhart looks something like a cross between a miniaturized Brazilian shanty town made of pressed sawdust, and some strange industrial-size object boxed and boarded up ready for shipment. But that's only from the outside. You step through one of the false doorways, and you're halfway along a dingy, carpeted corridor, lit by oil lamps, with windows that look out vaguely towards backcloths of formal gardens or Scottish hills. Reaching one end and turning around to look back along the diminishing, smoky corridor, the effect is undeniable. It's a trench. The bell rings. Silence. It's the middle of the night. A door opens. A perplexed and sorry-looking patient shuffles out of his room, wrapped in a white sheet, and tries the door of the bathroom. Another man opens his bedroom door, sees the ghostly apparition and scurries back to bed. At the far end of the corridor, like a man at the wrong end of a telescope, Sassoon emerges from his room, dressed in slippers, flannelette pyjamas and a dressing-gown tied at the waist. He peers along the now empty passageway, murmurs the word 'madness' to himself, and retreats. 'Cut,' somebody bawls. The bell rings twice, and the director, Gillies MacKinnon, hops out of his director's chair and scoots off down the hallway for a directorial word in Wilby's ear, before they try the whole thing again.

'I watch it all on a monitor now, as we're shooting it,' he tells you between takes, as the oil lamps are being topped up and Make-up are reapplying the bags under Wilby's eyes. Whenever the camera stops rolling, dozens of hired-hands swarm on to the set like mechanics in the pit lane at Silverstone, the most welcome of them being the man who wheels in and cranks up the instant heating system – space-age gas-burners that roar like two jet-propelled hair-driers. 'Otherwise, there's too much going on, and the camera-man's the only one who knows what it looks like.' MacKinnon seems completely in control, very much on top of things without having to crack the whip, and you get the feeling that respect and admiration are the motivating factors for most of the people milling around here, and a belief in his vision of the finished film. We chat about some of the problems of bringing film and poetry together – mainly the way in which pictures can rob poetry of its power, and the difficulty of providing an image which isn't simply an illustration of the words being said. Certainly it isn't just a case of splicing the two together and imagining that the whole will be greater than the sum of its parts. Maybe it's for this reason that the film contains no more than a couple of dozen lines of Owen's and Sassoon's poetry in total. Maybe that's enough. MacKinnon jumps up into his director's chair, buttons up his tatty combat jacket against the cold, stares into the monitor, and the man in the white sheet goes back to his mark.

James Wilby's retreat isn't so much a five-star Winnebago with water-bed and mini-bar, as an actual two-berth caravan with a formica kitchenette and foldaway bunk, more suited to a camp-site above Morecambe Bay than the wings of a four-million-dollar film set. Over a flask of coffee and innumerable roll-ups, he tells you that he didn't think he'd get the part of Sassoon because he doesn't look like him. He's mistaken. With his hair pushed back under the peak of his officer's cap and with his Merchant–Ivory English face, he looks disturbingly like the classic cameo portrait of Sassoon that many people would recognize. It's the face of a low-ranking royal or some wrong-side-of-the-blanket aristocrat. There's also an intensity and a pressure about Wilby, a sense of something being kept under control, held back by propriety and correctness.

'I think there's some spiritual good right at the heart of Sassoon,' he says, lighting up again.

'Will he stay with you, afterwards?' you ask him.

'Yes. They all do.'

'Who were you playing last?'

'Another gay officer – but quite different.'

'And next?'

'Nobody, thank God.'

'Did you write poems yourself, when you were younger?'

'Yes. But I gave it up because I couldn't do it.'

He flicks ash into the ashtray and blows smoke at the bare bulb on the ceiling. You're trying to explore some common ground between actors and poets, but not really getting anywhere. The lunch gong rings, and just before you duck out through the caravan door, Wilby says, 'It's not really an anti-war film, you know.' Your guess is that it's difficult to know when an actor is working and when he's off duty, and I'm not sure if this is Wilby in role recalling Sassoon's line, 'I can't say no war is ever justified,' or telling you in an actorly way that James Wilby is a bit of a fighter.

You catch up with Stuart Bunce over a school-dinner sponge pudding and custard in the dining-room (portacabin) next to the cafeteria (hot-dog van). Smaller than Wilby, more smiley and less worked-up, it's apparent by this time that the casting department have definitely got it right, not just in terms of looks and stature but also with status and attitude. Owen was brought up in the backstreets of Birkenhead by financially ruined parents, an upbringing in contrast to Sassoon's background of hunting, golfing and privately published collections of verse. You don't know where Bunce grew up, but with his tie off-centre and his collar not quite straight, he has the undeniable look of Paul McGann in *The Monocled Mutineer*.

'I read Owen at school,' he says, 'like most people did I suppose. But I never thought . . . well, I never thought I'd be him!'

'What sort of things help you get into character?'

'When there's a shot of me writing, I try to fill in some of the blanks in the unfinished poems. And I practise his signature.'

'Which hand did he write with?'

'Er . . . oh, shit.'

He's kidding. He knows. Bunce also talks about the responsibility of playing a real person rather than an imagined one, almost as though he were saving Owen from the fiction of history through some sort of dramatic resurrection.

'Is the script being filmed chronologically?' you ask him, having run out of poet-asks-actor-playing-poet-what-it's-like questions.

'No, I'm already dead,' he grins. 'After lunch there's a bit with Rivers in the corridor. Come and watch.'

In the script it's listed as SC.49 INT. CORRIDOR – NIGHT, and contains five lines of dialogue, none of them longer than half a dozen words. You start thinking that you might be home by teatime, but three hours and several takes later you're still watching a minutely adjusted version of the same scene, with Rivers apologizing to Owen for shouting, and Owen inquiring as to the health of his room-mate. It should be a drag, but it's fascinating, with Pryce timing his silences and the modulation of his voice to perfection, and Bunce sputtering and stuttering his lines like somebody with terminal hiccups blowing out birthday candles. It's almost as if it's Pryce the actor rather than Rivers the doctor that Bunce is reacting to, and makes you think that Pryce might be one of the few overpaid superstars in the film world that actually earns his corn. His performance is so immaculate and his presence on the set so powerful that I don't even mind when he doesn't want to be interviewed.

'He's a bit crabby,' explains one of the puffa jackets.

'Today, you mean, or all the time?'

'Oh, just with *Evita* and everything.'

You can see that it must be a fag, having to meet a living poet just because you're in a film with two dead ones, so you don't blame him. In any case, the bell rings for the end of filming, and after a little bit of agonizing by the director, it's agreed that you can be the first outsider to watch a few snatches of the finished product, 'bearing in mind that this is very early stages'.

These days, editing seems to be done on a computer screen rather than something more romantic, and you wonder at first if it's going to be like watching the Nintendo version of *Regeneration*. No such thing. A camera inches along a narrow, black passageway towards a point of light at the far end. There's a ripple of water as something scurries away, and a dripping noise, and the impression of brickwork. It's a canal. A tunnel. At the far end there's something like a fallen tree or a car crash or a pile of rubbish. The camera comes out into daylight, moves forward. It's a pile of uniforms. No, it's a heap of bodies, half-submerged, torn, broken, bloody. The camera moves forward. Skin, hands. A face, upside-down, quite dead. It's Owen. Bunce, you mean. No, you mean Owen. The camera waits.

'Show him the trenches,' says MacKinnon, sat behind you.

More of the same, shot from above this time. Aerial. Cartographical. It looks like artwork made with human remains, then a ploughed field fertilized with corpses, or the dead erupting from patches of earth. Andy Goldsworthy meets Damien Hirst. It looks like more dead than we thought we could manage, then more. Rain. A trench full of soldiers, all dead. More soldiers, just sleeping. More soldiers covered with blankets, dead. Too hard to watch, too hard not to. Birdsong. Sassoon and another man running without sound. Gunfire. The other man with a hole through his head. Dead. And so on.

Someone says, 'We were filming at eleven o'clock on 11th November, and stopped for the two-minute silence, with the actors in their uniforms, stood in a trench.' Nobody needs to say what that must have been like, and nobody does. You watch a few more scenes involving Owen, Sassoon and Rivers, all disturbingly good, then collect your little press-pack and goody-bag before exiting through a back door into Glasgow.

All this leads to other things, other thoughts. You were a student in Portsmouth when the fleet went past the end of the road, making for the South Atlantic. They wouldn't have asked, but if they had have done, would you have gone? You might have. You were young enough. Dumb enough. Didn't have much else to do at the time. You were watching football on the telly at home when the game-show hosts masquerading as CNN journalists announced the beginning of the Gulf War from a hotel bedroom in Baghdad. Would you have gone? Probably not. You were too clever by then, too cool, too *against*.

Now you're thirty-three with a wonky spine, so the question probably won't come up again, and even if it did, it's hard to imagine yourself or any English poet these days putting him or herself in the firing line, bringing back first-hand poetic accounts from the front. Tony Harrison might have been flown in to Bosnia to send poems home to the *Guardian*, but it's not really the same thing, is it, and maybe War Poetry, in that sense, is a thing of the past. All the poets you know are too smart, too bolshy and too shit-scared to go anywhere near that kind of action. It's not a criticism. Anyway, what good would we be in the modern theatre of war, unless one of the warheads needed a greeting message writing on it, or a computer needed plugging in? The Fourth World War, maybe, but poets will be sitting out the next one, with conscripts being press-ganged from video arcades and cyber-cafés, not from writing workshops or the mailing list of *Poetry Review*.

On the way home you begin replaying another clip from the film.

It's the scene from *Regeneration* when Rivers visits the National Hospital in London, to meet Dr Yealland and observe his pioneering work in dealing with the psycho-neuroses of war.

In the 'electrical room', the patient, Callan, has conductive pads attached to his back and neck, and a probe is inserted into his mouth.

Yealland: 'I'm going to lock the door when the orderlies have gone. You will talk before you leave. It is the only way out. Do you understand? There is no alternative.'

Yealland flicks a switch and a current flows into the patient's throat. Each time he fails to respond with speech, the voltage is stepped up. Time passes. An hour. Two hours. The electrical probe is disconnected, then reconnected to the larynx. The voltage is increased. The patient twists in agony. Yealland bellows theatrical encouragement from his position by the switch. Rivers cannot watch. More voltage. Callan rigid with pain. The hiss of electricity through flesh. Eventually a sound, a grunt, a word ('stop' – not good enough), other words, numbers, the days of the week. Callan is unstrapped, like Frankenstein's monster, and led away, cured.

Thinking it through again, you reach a point where you can't remember if it was Rivers who couldn't bear to watch any more, or you. You then begin to wonder whether you actually saw the scene at all – it was so vivid, profound, personal, authored – remembering it is more like remembering a passage from a book than a clip from a movie.

Next day, back in Marsden, you wander along to the park, and stand in front of the War Memorial with its two lions guarding the stone monument.

IN PROUD AND
THANKFUL MEMORY OF
THE MEN OF MARSDEN
WHO FELL IN THE
GREAT WAR

You read the names – gold wording against grey marble. W. Armitage, no relation. Two more in the next war. Three Bamforths, two Buckleys, one Dyson, one Hoyle, three Kewleys, one Norcliffe. Four Sykeses. Four Varleys.

IN HONOUR OF
THOSE WHO FOUGHT
IN SYMPATHY WITH
THOSE WHO SUFFERED
AND IN REMEMBRANCE OF
THOSE WHO FELL IN THE
GREAT WAR

Next night, Sheffield, you're doing a reading in a cinema, and you've been asked to talk about and present your favourite film in the second half, as a kind of double bill i.e. to get an audience. It isn't your favourite film, but you like *Kes* a lot, and it seems like a good thing to be going on about in South Yorkshire, even this many years after it was made. You begin with all the film-as-boil-in-the-bag-book stuff you've said elsewhere, then throw some other ingredients into the pan.

For instance, that most films are mainstream, by which we mean American mainstream, which should be guarded against. A quick splash in the prevailing current can be just what you need on a Saturday night in front of the telly or at the flicks, but why can't we tap into our own channels rather than diving head-first into someone else's dirty water? Secondly, film can't do metaphor. It can do extended metaphor, or conceit, or symbolism, or meaning, but it can't bring about those moments of electrical comprehension that we get in literature, based on likeness or similitude or comparison.

Kes rises above all that, somehow. For one thing, it happens to be better than the book, which isn't to take anything away from Barry Hines's *A Kestrel for a Knave*, but the screen version simply transcends it. One reason is its cast of somebodies and nobodies, particularly the nobodies, and especially David Bradley, playing Casper. All characters are compromised by the identity of an actor; the more famous the actor, the greater the compromise, until the point is reached where the actor is actually compromised by the character, poor thing. In a book, though, a character isn't 'played' by anyone. In *Kes*, Billy Casper is Billy Casper is Billy Casper, not Macaulay Culkin, not even David Bradley, because we don't know who David Bradley is, before or after. There's a purity here not broken by images of other films and other lives. A purity, and a democracy also.

Another reason for the film's success is that it gets beyond the northern realism that most projects of its type set as their limit of achievement. *Kes* creates a universe somewhere between heaven and hell, where hell is the prospect of the coal-pit and heaven the flight of a wild bird through living daylight. Casper the urchin as Casper the angel, practising the most arcane and noble of activities – falconry – in that space between the slag-heap of his circumstances and the realm of his imagination, his only true freedom.

It's almost time to let it roll. You remind everyone of the broken wall, like a cliff-face, where Casper climbs and lifts the bird from its nest. Drive down the M1 near Barnsley, look to the left, and it's still there, crumbling away, like a monument to the film. You make the point that this could be Yorkshire's answer to Disneyland – a pile of stones seen from a motorway – and hope that it stays that way. You make the point that in these parts, 'the movies' can be something more than popcorn and baseball hats and films that begin with the New York skyline and end with a smoking gun, and that cinema can be something nearer the mark, closer to home. You look up, and in and amongst an audience of seventy heads that are nodding in agreement, notice about a dozen goatee beards and baseball caps, unmoved, that aren't.

Over the Top into Lancashire

To Rochdale, to read a poem commissioned by the Co-operative Society to celebrate their 150th birthday. The main festivities are taking place in the town hall, that great pile of stone squatting on the 'Esplanade', looking like something that made an emergency landing in Lancashire while making for Austria or Germany. Rumour has it that the town hall was high on Hitler's list of buildings to be spared attention by the *Luftwaffe*, presumably because he fancied it as a northern administration centre or wanted to hear Wagner played on the massive organ, rather than having his eye on it as a country retreat. His orders were obviously followed to the letter, although the special agents who infiltrated the region via the town-planning office made a first-class job of decimating the surrounding area. They carry on working for the same cause today, unaware that the war came to an end over fifty years ago.

A commissioned poem is a strange thing, especially when the commissioning agents are known to be careful savers rather than carefree shopaholics. This doesn't mean that the huddle of northern businessmen who proposed the deal in the boardroom of their Manchester headquarters were a bunch of tight-fisted skinflints; far from it. But 'value for money' was an issue on the agenda, and certain facial expressions made it pretty clear that in this particular instance the 'less is more' principle that often characterizes contemporary poetry need not apply. The odd rhyme wouldn't be a bad thing either, particularly at the end lines.

The other peculiarity about a commissioned poem is the troubling notion that somebody might read it, quite a few somebodies in fact, people who don't read many poems but funnily enough have a pretty firm concept of what one should look like. Ideally, it ought to say what it means and mean what it says, rather than beating about the bush or going round the houses, and it ought to get to the point. Otherwise, what's the point? To help the commissioned poet stick to the task in hand, the Co-op make available a wad of documents and photographs, including a fading picture of the instigators of the Co-operative Movement, thirteen of them sitting around a table like Christ and his apostles in the famous paintings of the infamous meal. Either that, or an early Rugby-League team.

On the day of the reading, the Territorial Army have been enlisted to patrol the town centre and prevent unwanted visitors getting anywhere near the main event in their vehicles. A man in a camouflage jacket, track-suit bottoms and brown Doc Martens sticks his toy gun into the car and asks to see 'some paperwork'. He talks coded gibberish into his walkie-talkie before the person at the other end obviously asks him what the hell he's on about, then he lifts the traffic cone from the middle of the road and points to the car park at the side of the town hall. Helium balloons are escaping into the galaxy. A helter-skelter spits children on to the pavement, like cherry stones. Inside, the local brass band finish their first set, the good and the great of Lancashire look up from under their British Home Stores hats or over the top of their programmes, and a man from the wrong side of the border walks out into the spotlight, ready to co-operate.

Provision

Picture this: a baker's dozen of them,
thirteen of the first co-operators, men

assembled for the last unwholesome supper
of costly bread, extortionate butter,

sick to death of forking out good money for old rope,
small beer, tough cheese, spilt milk, tail end, soft soap.

Good eggs;
their heads

together had a vision of the equitable
trade of animal and mineral and vegetable,

and instead of lining purses, pockets,
scattering like seeds the profits,

ploughing back each pound and penny
then dividing up the yield by many.

That was then, way back when,
but out of acorns . . . branches that extend

beyond the bounds of spending, earning,
into planning, sharing, showing, learning,

arms that stretch to give what's best
for getting going, growing, rest,

roots that are sunk to the salt of the earth;
fruits that flower, leaves of promise, worth.

Attractive terms;
happy returns.

Over the Top into Lancashire

It goes to show, plainly,
what the world should know, namely:

yesterday, today, tomorrow, how a corporation
can incorporate a good deal of co-operation.

From Salford to Jericho

Extracts from *From Salford to Jericho – Living on the Streets of Manchester*, Radio 4, 8 January 1996.
Voices by *Big Issue* vendors.
Produced by Kate Rowland.

Commission: poems to be written from the point of view of passers-by, debating whether or not to give money. This is the big issue. Poems to take their cue from documentary interviews with magazine vendors and other people sleeping rough in Manchester.

*

Claire: I was in school for about two weeks, and I come back out of it because I've not got my uniform. I miss my brother, he lives with his dad. Living in a house I can draw with my pencil crayons and sit down. Being on the streets it's sometimes cold and everyone just ignores me when I'm speaking to my mum when my mum's begging. Everyone just ignores you.

> Oh mister, mister, won't you pity me
> with my daughter lost in the world?
> Sorry no can do, I can't pity you
> but I'll buy some brains for the girl:

so off they tripped, to Dillons and Smiths,
for books on every subject under the sun,
and the daughter studied each one.

Claire: There was this person who was called Jeff, who bought me nearly £150 of books. He was teaching me German. German books, maths books, English . . .

Oh mister, mister, won't you teach me
with my daughter, lost in the world?
I can't teach you, sorry no can do,
but I'll buy some togs for the girl:

so off they marched, to Marks and Sparks,
for a winter coat that was second to none,
and the daughter kept it on.

Oh mister, mister, won't you dress me
with my daughter, lost in the world?
I'm afraid I can't, I haven't got the heart
but I'll buy some nosh for the girl:

so off went them to the Little Yang Sing,
for chicken chow mein and battered prawn balls
and the daughter scoffed it all.

Claire: I get up about eight, sometimes quarter past nine, and get ready, come downstairs, wake my mum up, tell her to get ready and come to town . . .

Oh mister, mister, won't you feed me
with my daughter, lost in the world?
No dear heart, I'm afraid I can't
but I'll buy some fun for the girl:

so they went on the bus, to Toys 'R' Us,
and rode in a trolley through the aisles of shelves
and the daughter helped herself.

Oh mister, mister, won't you treat me
with my daughter, lost in the world?
No my love, I wish that I could
but I'll show the world to the girl:

so they climbed to the top of the CIS block,
and gawped at a view that was full to the brim
and the daughter drank it in.

Claire: Sometimes I bring my pencil crayons down and draw, and sometimes I go into the church, and if I was going anywhere else I'd tell my mum. And sometimes I play with this girl called Fay, and her mum's a beggar as well.

Oh mister, mister, why pity her
when her mother sits here in the cold?
Because, my sweet, when you took to the street,
you stole two things that I owned:

a wife like you I can take or leave,
but my heart goes out to the girl.
And I lost that girl to the world.

*

Jay: I'll give you one instance, right, I was sleeping rough in a doorway, the same doorway that I'd been arrested in for sleeping in, and I was bedding down for the night, putting my cardboard down, putting my blankets out and all that, and a bunch of lads walked past me, been out on the beer, in the club, right, round the corner, and one of them shouted, 'I'm going home to mi nice warm house and mi nice warm bed . . .'

From Salford to Jericho

It was Mick's twenny first, we was out on the town;
we'd been in the Lamb and the George and the Crown
and the Cock and the Bull and the Hare and Hounds.
I was out of mi skull. We'd been pouring it down.

We was outside the Arndale, arsin around
when I seen this scruff in the door of a shop.
Like a sack of potatoes he was, gone off. So we stopped
and went over and had a good look and a laugh.

I hate all that. Fungus, they are, make mi sick.
Some of em there with their dogs and their kids,
beggin for brass for a drink or a fix.
And some of em stink. Put mi right off mi chips,

this one did. So I couldn't resist. I said
I'm going home to mi nice warm house and mi nice warm bed,
and we all fell about thinking we was alright
and that he was outside for the night.

I was walking away from him, just turned mi back
when he tries to come out with some smart-arse crack
It will be nice and warm
because I've been sleeping with your missis
about havin my lass in the sack so I'm thinking
I'm not having that, not from a scumbag like him.

I've got O'levels me. I've got four. Alright, three.
I work ten hours a day. Six days a week.
I don't have to listen to that kind of crap
from a rag-arse like him dossin down in the street,

on the scrounge, on the dole. So I told him
to button his trap, crawl back in his hole
if he wanted to live, if he knew what was good
for his health. He was brickin himself,

I could tell. I'd have hammered im into the dirt
but I din't want his blood on mi fifty quid shirt
and mi sixty quid shoes and mi ninety quid kecks.
Good clobber, this, from Top Shop and Next.

He said something else that I missed, but mi mates said
oh leave him to sleep in his shit and his piss,
so I left him to stew. I've got O'levels, me.
I've got three. Alright, two.

I see him in town all the time, him and his type,
down and out, no bottle, no spine.
I think oi, get a life, get a job, get a house,
get a wife. Like me, mi old sunshine, like mine.

Jay: That was his head done in, he started saying I'll do this and do that, I said come back next week when you're big enough, and his mates just pulled him back, and said you deserved it sort of thing.

*

James: I think it was a vicar once said, that I think was quite good, that if you give 50p to every beggar on the street and one out of the ten people you give to was really in need, and needed something to eat, then that's a good thing. So I think that's a good way of looking at it. I mean, there's a lot of people out there who are in need.

Davy: I sell the Issue outside Kendal's. I can't understand how someone can go in there and pay £150 for a bottle of perfume, then come out and not give 75p for a magazine.

The house of God has many regions,
many parishes and states.
More chambers than the heart,
more strength than bricks and beams and slates.

The thumbs and fingers, pressed together,
pointing skyward, make a prayer.
Prised open at the palms they make a roof
with room for everyone and everywhere.

A man of God cannot withstand
the image of an open hand,
a man of God cannot withhold
the gift of part of what he owns,
when called.

Of all the coins, one coin means more.
Not sovereign like the pound,
not even gold, not milled, not copper, bronze, not round,
but silver of a type, and seven-sided,
one for every act of mercy,
symbol of the hungry, naked, ailing,
lifeless, captive, homeless, thirsty.

In a street communion of a sort
I hand the metal obols out,
one heptagon for every outstretched arm,
for every upturned hat,
not in remembrance of the Lord,
not flesh and blood
but in the name of bread and soup, or drink, or drugs,
whatever fills the hole, whatever feeds the soul.

Remember, one man's poison is another's meat.
Remember, one man's porridge is another's feast.

I think of those without possessions of their own
the meekest of the meek, inheriting the earth
or passing through the needle's eye of heaven, forth
from Bolton into Bethlehem,

from Bury into Nazareth,
from Rochdale into Galilee,
from Salford into Jericho,
from Patricroft into Jerusalem, I say again

a man of God cannot resist
that begging bowl below the wrist,
must give, must lean, bend at the hips
and load each hand as if it were a balance, till the balance
    tips.

The house of God has many regions,
many parishes and states.
More chambers than the heart,
more strength than bricks and beams and slates.

The thumbs and fingers, pressed together,
pointing skyward, make a prayer.
Prised open at the palms they make a roof
with room for everyone, and everywhere.

*

*Smithy: There was a man wrote in the paper that he made £125 a
day begging and selling the Issue, but you can't make that money,
you're lucky if you make £20 a day, and you're there at it in the rain
and the snow, and he's started saying he's made £125, that's why the
public get fed up, because they're working Monday to Friday for
maybe £140 a week, trying to save up to go on holiday . . .*

In the old days they were more in the country than in the
towns and cities, and they wore boots and hats and big coats
with string tied round and ate berries and plants.

They carried everything they owned in a blanket knotted to the end of a stick and they called you sir or mam and we called them gentlemen of the road, or tramps.

When we lived on the farm they'd come to the back door for a bowl of pea soup and ham-shank or a cooking apple if they'd rather.

They came in the Spring, when the weather changed, and went to Spain or Africa like birds in the winter, according to father.

They didn't wash unless it rained, so they smelt like vase-water after a week or an umbrella left overnight to dry.

They were old, with hair down to their shoulders and beards to their belts, and they lived peacefully under the blue roof of the sky.

But these days if you walk down Deansgate or Oxford Road or under the colonnade past the Town Hall,

or look in the doorways in Cross Street and St Ann's Square, or stroll at ten at night back to the car after a film or a show, there's some poor wretch living like a snail or a rat in every hole.

I used to keep a few pence in my glove when I was shopping to treat the odd one to a sandwich or a cup of tea.

If I buy that magazine, *The Big Picture*, I can't take it home, because Donald, my husband, says that some of them make up to a hundred pounds a day or more, tax free.

I'd prefer to give food and clothes than money they might use for drink or cigarettes or that sort of thing,

but when I did buy one of them a hot dog one day he said

he was a vegetarian. I thought – you can't win.

Another time, I was fishing around in my purse to give one of them a fifty-pence piece, when his mobile phone went off in his pocket. It beggars belief. Actually, I have to confess,

those things happened to a friend of a friend of mine, not to me personally, so might not be true in the strictest sense.

Jason: I'm not scared, but I am worried . . . like . . . this lad that's just been killed, this Michael, he was one of us, you know what I mean, it didn't scare me, it shocked me, but I was just thinking . . . like . . . that could have been me. Everyone's vulnerable, aren't they? Even in your house you're vulnerable. It's like we're just more vulnerable than yous. We're only a couple of steps away from where you are.

Over the Top into Lancashire

December, the annual Yorkshire Avalanche Dodgers walk to Diggle
for dinner in a pub and a few pints on the way back, on one of
those four unnameable days between Boxing Day and New Year's
Eve. We meet at ten in the morning, two dozen of us outside
Pule Side Working Men's Club on the edge of the valley and
set off into the snow above the village. There's a metallic-blue sky,
and a tangerine sun turning the landscape pale orange. Underfoot,
the paths across the moor are frozen streams of ice, like stretch
marks, with a dusting of snow on top, and every third or fourth
stride goes through the crust into the marsh-grass and bog-water
underneath, which for some reason is warm. It's like walking
across a great body asleep under a street light at dawn, the skin
only just tight enough to keep us from sinking into the flesh
beneath.

We follow the ley-line of the old packhorse road, built by Blind
Jack of Knaresborough, somehow, then curve off to a summit on
the left to look at the view in front and the distance behind. The
cigarettes come out, and a thermos, and five or six silver hip-flasks
that catch the sun and flash messages across the Pennines. Over
there it's Lancashire. Somewhere beneath us, trains shuttle through
one of the world's longest tunnels, their diesel fumes rising through
the air shafts that once drew steam up through the hills and
into the clouds. Spiracles. Geysers. Stories of stones toppled into
the endless holes from above, or was it sheep? Stories of men
riding horses or driving cars through the tunnel when the road

was closed with snow, seeing a light up ahead. Stories of the witches' coven at the midway point, pentangles drawn on the wall, the horns of goats, a candle that never goes out.

One man sets a camera on a stone then sprints back for a group photograph, probably in the same place as last year, and the year before that. Another man produces a satellite navigator – a black oblong handset with a digital readout – and we all huddle round to inspect the device that can pin-point the latitude and longitude and altitude of the man carrying it to within ten metres. Its owner flips open the front cover, pulls out the aerial with his teeth, presses a button with his thumb, and tells us our exact position on the surface of the earth.

A man with a compass isn't impressed. Another man knows the spot-height of one of the hills to the north, in yards, and looking along the eye-line of his outstretched arm, reckons it's about right.

For yourself, you can't help thinking how useless it is without a map, and even then it wouldn't be much good in fog or a blizzard, without something to point in a particular direction. Ten metres might as well be ten miles in these parts when the cloud comes down, and being lost and knowing where you are can amount to the same thing in certain circumstances. It's getting to where you aren't that counts. As for the altitude function, is it a comfort to know that you're about to perish at five-thousand feet? Or when the boat starts to capsize, you flick the switch of your hi-tech gizmo, only to be told you're at sea-level.

You once flew to Japan for about two-hundred pounds with an airline that must have had the first option on Aeroflot's decommissioned planes. The flight took twelve hours, and instead of showing films, the one television set ran a video of a cartoon aeroplane making its way across the world, in actual time, towards a flag on the other side of the screen. Like watching a snooker ball taking all day to roll the length of the table and into a pocket, or an infinitely slow putt on a golf green. After about three hours, a man behind you shouted GET IN THE HOLE!

Probably you'd be more sympathetic towards the satellite navigator if you weren't packing your bags tomorrow and setting off for a place in the Amazon Basin that doesn't appear on any map and doesn't exist according to the Brazilian Embassy in London. The trip – one of those exercises in travelling as far away as possible from what you know and where you live – all hinges on teaming up with a gang of men on the bank of the great river, and sailing upstream, further than the small towns of Safety and Comfort, past the trading-post of Knowledge and the tiny settlement of Certainty, and on into forest, beyond the last light of Experience. It's presumably for that reason, and the fact that the gadget we're all gawping at falls short of the radar-tracking-system-cum-matter-transporter which might be of some use, that you're sniffy about it. You try to remember Auden's summary of the compass. 'North – cold, wind, precipices, glaciers, caves, heroic conquest of dangerous obstacles, whales, hot meat and vegetables, concentration and production, privacy. South – heat, light, drought, calm, agricultural plains, trees, rotarian crowds, the life of ignoble ease, spiders, fruits and desserts, the waste of time, publicity. West and East are relatively neutral. West is more favourable, i.e., more northern, but conjures up the unheroic image of retired couples holding hands in the sunset; East is definitely southern and means dried figs and scorpions.'

We sit around on the cairn on the peak of the hill, breath indistinguishable from smoke in the cold air. When a mobile phone goes off, it's an act of the most primitive magic, a voice from fifty miles away, perfectly formed, without cable or connection of any type, wishing a man on a mountain-top a merry Christmas and a happy New Year, right into his lug-hole. He might just as well be trusting in telepathy as wavelengths and digital information. The way that the great cosmologists model the universe – from their imaginations.

The phone call comes to an end. The man with the navigator shouts out our exact location again and slips the device back in his pocket. On the bridge of the USS *Enterprise*, the crew confirm our position, having beamed us down safely on to planet Earth in the last remaining days of 1996. We set our phasers on 'stun', and begin the slow, careful descent, into the other country.

In a Perfect World

Dawn in the jungle, on the equator, happens pretty quickly. They filmed some of the Global Sunrise project from the crown of a tree near here – they must have been up very early in the morning is all I can say. Where the sun comes up, vertically, like a bubble through a drink – that's due east. No question. And the cockerel whose clockwork has all gone haywire had to be dumped on the far side of the river by one of the Indians, so it's quiet this morning. I unzip the fly-net and stroll out on to the wooden planks of the mollucca. Parrots, in pairs, glide from the far bank to a tall Brazil nut tree at the back of the camp, and a single freshwater dolphin jumps through the hoop of its own ripple twenty yards downstream. It's heaven, of course, but a long way from home. You'd just be making the first brew of tea – Earl Grey and PG Tips in the same pot – and pulling the curtains back, flicking the switch for Radio 4 to see who's died or Radio 5 for the sport. And ripping open the mail for your two favourite types of post – straight in the bin or straight in the bank. Then back to bed for half an hour with the paper or a book. Wait for the water to warm up.

Lucy, a fifteen-foot cayman, goes past like a nuclear sub. They say it's safe to take a dip, but tell that to the dog that Lucy dragged from the riverbank and downed in one gulp. The time of day, told by the height of the sun, is ten or eleven o'clock. I don't eat breakfast as a rule, but wander down to the makeshift jetty with a hard-boiled egg left over from last night's meal, and strong coffee in a tin cup. They say all the sacred rivers in this neck of the woods begin with an X, and this is the Xishuau. It runs south to the Jauaperi, which empties into the Rio Negro, which decants into the Amazon, which steers a course for the ambushed city of Manaus – but that's a three-day sail with a good crew in a good boat, and still a thousand miles from the coast. Might as well make the most of this once-in-a-lifetime trip while it lasts. Besides, you'd only be trundling into town, Huddersfield town, to the Blue Rooms Café for a round of toast, or sat in the buffet car between Wakefield Westgate and King's Cross, or looking bemused at a sheet of paper or computer screen, staring into space.

Over the back of the secret lake, through the flooded forest, there's a small plantation with bananas and all the rest of it growing wild. Jaua's building a new hut for himself because the old place is spooked. Valdamar cooks something to eat – rainbow bass, spit-roast on a fire of twigs and sticks. He's got a ghetto-blaster, a pile of batteries from God knows where, and nine kids. Midday, the sun's directly overhead, like a thought. There's a catfish snared on a loose line that needs to be reeled in and cleaned. We're taking canoes upstream for the night, so I pack a bag with a toothbrush and a few clothes, then get my head down for half an hour's kip, and dream. It's a dream that travels several thousand miles to the door of a house. Stepping out, you can walk most of the reservoirs around Marsden in an afternoon, if you pick up your feet. Butterley, Blakeley, Wessenden, Wessenden Head; over to Swellands, Black Moss, Redbrook, then follow the skyline to March Haigh, Cupwith, drop down the valley to Tunnel End, Sparth, then up the other side to Deer Hill. The Riverhead Tap, Marsden's brew pub, is a variation on the same theme. Sparth Mild, Black Moss Stout, March Haigh Bitter, abv 4.6. It's open all day.

There are eight of us in three canoes. I say canoes, but they're really scooped-out logs with a point at both ends. We're 30 per cent of the population for a thousand square miles, and probably more besides. Hottest part of the day, mid-afternoon. I've got a solar-powered watch – it's doing cartwheels and looping the loop. Chris, who owns the reserve, is naming the rivers and inlets and mounds. Literally, this is uncharted ground. I stick my oar in, and christen a natural clearing in the trees Crown Green, and think of how it might look as a lawn, with neat green grass cropped to an inch of its life. What is it, Friday afternoon? Call it a day, call it a week. You might just have finished a poem, or even a book. Stick the bowls in the back of the car, go for a game with the old boys in the park. Late summer, the woods running well. Tea in the hut. The sound of lignum vitae bumping against itself. Plenty of talk. Plenty of telling the tale.

I like the river here because it isn't land. Land is snakes, cover, bugs, ticks, visibility seven or eight yards, not being able to see the trees for the wood. River is open, breeze, view, and also food. Valdamar passes me one of the rods, and I pull out a small piranha with a home-made hook. He stuns it with a wooden club, chops out the mouthpart and holds it up. Not great eating, piranha; fiddly bones, flesh like mud, vinegar blood. Not a bad light meal before a game of five-a-side, though, which is where you'd be between eight and nine o'clock tonight. The ball comes loose in defence, and you tidy it up. You beat one man, nutmeg a second, play a wall-pass with the wall and lash a half-volley past the 'keeper just inside the right-hand post. He doesn't even move. Sweet as a nut. That's your hat trick, and the whistle goes.

Then what? What then? Manchester or Leeds, and the milk-train home or the all-night bus? A big Chinese meal with all your friends in the whole world and a lazy-Susan spinning the dishes to all corners of the room? A gallon at Pule Side Working Men's Club? A film? A party in the garden, booze keeping cool in the fish pond, whatever lights your candle in the summer-house, loud music at full blast till a cockerel croons in the last line of the last waltz to tell you it's dawn? It's a far cry. *I'm miles away. Daylight – last seen sinking without trace, due west. It's so dark you could cut it in slices and sell it as cake. It's the hell that you have to have to make heaven what it is. Valdamar checks under the hammocks for spiders and snakes. It's the rain forest, so it rains. Jaua keeps the fire going till it goes out. Howler monkeys shake the tops of trees and make their famous noise – like sheet metal being torn into strips. A jaguar sulks in the undergrowth. Don't go for a piss – take the wrong turn and it's next stop Peru, Ecuador, Guyana, or Columbia, via certain death. The perfect world turns a blind eye for the night. Nothing to do but hit the sack, lie still, wait for morning and paradise.*

Traffic News – Regional Updates

Driving along the M62 in freezing fog, visibility down to four or five yards. No one else on the road, or if there is, you can't see them. Up ahead, there's a sign with a message flashing on it. You crawl towards it, and just about come to a halt trying to read it. It says FOG.

Driving along the middle lane of the M62 doing about eighty. A car goes past on the outside doing about ninety. The driver has a book propped open on the steering wheel, and he's reading it.

Driving along the M62 in the contraflow. A gang of men on the hard shoulder, mending the road. One of them lifts a long wooden pole out of a cauldron of bubbling tar, sets fire to it in the gas burner underneath, then brings the flaming end of the pole up towards his face, and lights his cigarette. Then he tosses the pole back into the tar and picks up his spade, puffing away on the cigarette, without having touched it.

Directory Enquiries I

February. The telephone rings.
　'Mr Armitage?'
　'Yes.'
　'It's Direct Line Insurance in Leeds. Is it right you're a poet?'
　'Yes.'
　'Are you well known?'
　'How do you mean?'
　'Are you famous?'
　'Er . . . have *you* heard of me?'
　'No.'
Silence. The sound of thinking.
　'OK, thanks.'

Directory Enquiries II

March. The telephone rings.

'Mr Armitage?'

'Yes.'

'It's Direct Line Insurance in Leeds.'

'Oh yes.'

'You're not a probation officer any more, are you?'

'I'm not.'

'You're a poet, aren't you?'

'I am.'

'I'm afraid there's an eighty-two-pound loading for that.'

'How come?'

'Higher-risk category.'

'Higher risk than a probation officer?'

'That's right.'

'How come?'

'Entertainment and Leisure. The public – nutters and all that.'

'I see.'

'Sorry. Unless you want to explain to us what it is you do exactly, as a job?'

'You mean for money?'

'To earn a living.'

'Not really.'

'Fine. So will it be direct debit or shall we send you a bill?'

Huddersfield is Hollywood

It's official. Or rather Holmfirth is *Last of the Summer Wine* country, and Slaithwaite is Skelthwaite in I T V's *Where the Heart Is*, and Marsden, formerly Pickersgill of *Pickersgill People* non-fame, is *Wokenwell*, as well as being one of the suburbs of *Last of the Summer Wine* country.

On the one hand, this gives people in Huddersfield's outlying villages something to point at when they watch telly on a Sunday night. On the other, the fact that it's now easier to buy a Nora Batty pencil case or Compo teapot in Holmfirth than a loaf of bread is an indication that these things can go seriously wrong. The BBC's policy of dumbing-down *Last of the Summer Wine* as far as possible without moving it to a children's slot on Saturday morning has obviously paid off, and its intelligence-proof formula of REPETITION (X: 'He's bought a bike.' Y: 'What does he want a bike for?' Z: 'I had a bike once. A red one.' Y: 'I can't see what he wants one of them for. Not a bike.'), WARDROBE (the bike came in a job lot with a diving suit) and CONTRAPTION (the bike is gas-powered) means that even the most lobotomized and comatose of viewers can follow the plot without referring to subtitles on Ceefax. Coach parties of pilgrims jam the car park, crowd the teashops, stuff their faces, block the toilets. No one can remember the days when the programme was a minimalist existential dialogue written by Samuel Beckett.

In Marsden, the *Huddersfield Examiner* was right when it pointed out that 'not everyone welcomed ITV' when they turned up in their pantechnicons and tuck-wagons to turn the village into small-town Wokenwell, traffic chaos being the main reason, followed closely by the rudeness factor. 'You can't drive down here because we're filming' became a new catch-phrase, meaning a variety of things from 'Mind your own business,' to 'Not tonight I've got a headache.' 'Watch me' became the standard reply. Some locals stood in circles gawping at the action like hangers-on at a party or lonely kids on the edge of a game of football, waiting to be asked to play. The image of Nazi collaborators came to mind, but no one actually said it. Rumours went round. The Special Constables diverting vehicles away from Peel Street had no authority and no powers of arrest. Someone who'd rented out his premises as a set would never need to work again. In the Parochial Hall, Celia Imrie was still being filmed in the bath when the Operatic and Amateur Dramatic Society turned up to rehearse; one of the film crew scuttled off to the Conservative Club to hire out another venue for the displaced thespians, laughed at the pitiful price of renting the upstairs room, but still asked for a receipt for double the amount.

When *Wokenwell* finally hit the screens in early summer, it received a mixed reaction, especially from council binmen Colin Primus and Paul Wood. Vox-popped by the *Examiner*, Mr Primus said, 'It could have been a bit more exciting.' Mr Wood was more optimistic, saying, 'Given a chance, it'll probably pick up.'

Actually, the geography consultants in the Where Shall We Do This One departments of the production companies involved got it wrong by a factor of about ten miles when they stuck the pin in the map in the south-west sector of Huddersfield. Hebden Bridge, conveniently located amid charming woodland above Halifax, with excellent communication links to all centres of media activity, seems to be a much more plausible location for television drama, having everything that Wokenwinegillthwaite can offer, plus more. If this sounds like cheap flattery, made with the hope of luring the infestation of the film world out of the Colne Valley and into Calderdale – it is. But there's no need to be suckered into it by one man's casual speculations, when tonight Hebden Bridge is the star attraction on *Look North*'s mini-feature *Heartlands*, 'a look at the places and the people that make the region tick'. The presentation really focuses on the whirlpool of attitudes and forces at work in the town, represented in the red corner by the white Rastas and New Age druids in their caravan camp down by the canal (soundtrack: Alanis Morissette), and in the blue corner by Sir Bernard Ingham, Thatcher's one-time press-secretary, shown here huffing and puffing his way up 45-degree cobbled ginnels, mumbling things like '. . . why the hell should I work my b– fingers to the bone to keep them in the manner to which they've become accustomed?' and 'Pennine people are the original awkward squad, of which I count myself one.'

Ingham gives the impression of someone who dislikes the travellers not so much because of the mess he says they make, but because they're not locals, and therefore not entitled. What he thinks of a more permanent outsider, Sylvia Plath, buried in Heptonstall churchyard above the town, we don't learn. Plath's face appears on the screen, like a flag, followed by one of her conscripts changing flowers at the grave-side. This week, the stone contains the married name Hughes, occasionally missing, pecked off by hard-nosed supporters claiming Plath as one of their own. The biggest surprise as far as this part of the film is concerned is that the graveyard is free from practising poets. Lumb Bank, the residential writing centre on the side of the valley, is only ten minutes' walk away, and it's usual to find at least a couple of verse-mongers mooching around the headstones, trying to summon up the opening lines for their new sonnet 'At the Grave of Sylvia Plath', or variations on that theme.

During a drinks break at the barn dance in the Trade Hall,

Heartlands presenter Mike MacCarthy (blue-check shirt) asks one of the local musicians what it is that makes Hebden Bridge the Yorkshire Mecca for free-thinkers and free-movers. The musician tells him he's heard it said that Hebden is connected by ley-line to Glastonbury and Stonehenge.

MacCarthy: Do you think it's true?

Musician: No, I think it's a load of old bulldozers, myself.

Heartlands finishes with a trail of Hebden Bridgers filing off into the night, presumably to sacrifice a goat in Hardcastle Crags or offer prayers to the Mother Goddess from a crop-circle in the meadows. Back in the studio:

Sophie: What I want to know is, who was that blonde lady you were dancing with?

Mike: We'll talk about it later, Sophie. Moving swiftly on, here's Darren with the weather . . .

Jerusalem

*As the vine tree among the trees of the forest, which I have given to
the fire for fuel, so will I give the inhabitants of Jerusalem.* Ezekiel xv.6

Title Sequence

Early morning in the Calder Valley, a fingernail moon still hanging
in on its hook, the sky growing lighter. A heavy fog in the
depressions of the moorland landscape, like thick white smoke.

In the distance, a yellow pick-up van motors along a single-track
road and disappears into a hollow of mist. Silence, and then the
van is upon us, bursting up through the cloud and sweeping along
the winding road.

A few quick, jerky images from inside the cab of the van:
The Ride of the Valkyries playing at full tilt; a mouth below a
handlebar-moustache singing along, drowned out by the music;
one hand on the wheel, the other conducting the orchestra; a pair
of big wide-open eyes under a pelmet of heavy eyebrows, fixed on
the road ahead.

Outside, seen from a distance, the van comes to a stop above
a dark and narrow valley. Seen from behind, a tall man gets out,
and with the engine still running walks to the edge and looks
down over the canopy of trees. Mist hangs in the air; chimney
pots, aerials and satellite-dishes poke out curiously above the
treetops.

The camera begins a descent of the steep, wooded slope. The
first solid houses come into view, clinging to the gradient, improb-
ably two storeys high at the front, maybe six or seven at the

back, with ingenious pulley systems for hanging out washing or exercising pets, and elaborate chutes for rubbish disposal.

An attic room with a bare light-bulb reveals a New Age couple funnelling a large vat of liquid into small bottles. A textile mill converted into units reveals further signs of peculiar nocturnal entrepreneurship. Through one window, a glamour-photography session is in progress – a flashgun discloses naked flesh wrapped in a leopard-skin rug – then darkness again. Through another, a large man in overalls sits asleep, inches away from an ancient, clattering printing-press.

Further down, the trees clear to reveal the small and tidy premises of Jerusalem fire station, complete with a three-hole putting green on the lawn in front and a telephone-hatch in the wall. The camera goes in close to the telephone, pauses a moment, then follows the telephone cable down the wall and along the path to the gate of the fire station, where it plunges below ground and burrows its way across the street. We see worms, bones, coins, before emerging on the other side of the road with the cable and shooting up the wall of the Video Kabin opposite.

The cable takes a sharp right past Sugget & Sugget Gentlemen's Outfitters and The Pearl of India (Curry Yorkshire Puddings – Our Speciality) before looping itself elegantly on home-made telegraph poles in front of an unmanned railway station festooned with hanging baskets.

It resumes progress past parking meters and the indistinguishable shop-fronts of the Jerusalem Museum of Labour and Craft, and Conroy's General Hardware Store (est. 1882). Then it dives underground again, emerging after another journey through Jerusalem's unsung archaeological past in the taproom of The Hare and Hounds. On the window-sill there's a telephone. In the background, stretched out on a full-length snooker table, lies a sleeping fireman.

This peaceful scene is disturbed by the sound of an engine.

Reflected in the taproom window, the yellow van trundles by at a more sedate pace. Inside the van Wagner still blares, the same eyes observing Jerusalem's shopkeepers opening up for another day.

The shutters roll up on the butcher's to reveal a man in a blood-stained apron reaching inside a suspended carcass for his store of sausages, blood puddings and a float of money.

Through the tobacconist's window an elderly man dressed in jacket and tie weighs out loose tobacco.

At Jerusalem's second-hand-car showroom, a shabby man disappears inside carrying a sack with a woolly leg sticking out of it.

The van turns a corner into a terraced residential street. At the corner shop, Mr and Mrs Boot stand motionless side by side behind the counter, hands tucked under their aprons, waiting for the first customer of the day.

Halfway down the street the van stops. Wagner is silenced and the tall, well-built man gets out and unlocks the door of Number 27. He returns to the van and throws open the back doors to reveal a clutter of furniture and tea-chests.

Across the road at Number 28 a curtain on the top floor twitches.

From his bedroom window, John Edward Castle balefully surveys the arrival of Jerusalem's newest resident. Downstairs, peering from behind the nets, Rose Castle's heart beats faster . . .

Who's Who in Jerusalem

John Edward Castle, known as J E, is a man who enjoys power and influence, both in his own home and in the town. J E was a former station-master in the local fire service, but an accident at work left him incapacitated and housebound. The accident came about as a result of his near-suicidal bravery and heroism, looking for a child in a burning barn on Bonfire Night twenty-three years ago. From his bed, JE exerts control over his family, friends and acquaintances, and struggles to maintain his status, dignity and self-respect among the good people of the parish.

It's easy to feel sorry for JE because of his disability and his predicament, but his resourcefulness and ingenuity can take on the force of ruthlessness and corruption. His suggestions carry the weight of threats, and those who cross him are quick to be paid back in kind.

Communication is central to JE's regime. With the help of his side-kick, Softie, he uses every available gadget and gizmo to take his voice and his views into other houses, other lives. Trapped in the upstairs quarters of his tall and narrow terraced house, he 'talks' to the rest of the family through a tannoy system, with a loudspeaker placed strategically and symbolically on the mantelpiece in the front-room, above a roaring fire and beneath a portrait of the man himself in full fire-service uniform, complete with medals.

JE's tentacles extend into the homes of Jerusalem's other residents via a ramshackle, home-made crystal-set-cum-transmitting-device from which he broadcasts regularly to those willing to tune in. His opening gambit is always some cliché from the folklore of broadcasting, from 'Testing, Testing, One, Two, Three,' to 'Attention All Shipping, Attention All Shipping,' and even 'Germany calling, this is Germany calling.' On Saturday nights, JE excels himself, running a bingo session over the airwaves, calling out the numbers in the true spirit of the game, with the compliant Softie, equipped with mobile phone, out checking cards and delivering prizes on his moped. It's JE's dream to be elected Entertainments Secretary at Jerusalem Social Club, and to call out the numbers direct to the club by telephone link-up every weekend.

Balding, bespectacled, slightly flabby and usually sweating, JE is to be found propped up in bed in blue pyjamas, or rattling around his bedroom in a motorized wheelchair, dressing-gown and slippers.

Spoon, Jerusalem's ex-police inspector, returns to his old patch after the recent death of his wife, looking to put down anchor. Spoon and JE know each other of old. They lived in the same street, were in the same year at school. Quite simply, they detest each other.

Spoon was a hard man. His reappearance in Jerusalem opens old wounds. It was Spoon that pulled JE from the fire twenty-odd years ago ('Get that bleeding idiot out of there – messing up my paperwork'), striding into the flames in his police hat and shirtsleeves as the fire brigade looked on in oxygen masks and steamed-up goggles. Then in a perfunctory visit to the burns unit in Leeds (to rub salt in the wound, and gloat about his commendation) he found the woman he'd been waiting to meet all his life. It was John Edward's wife, Rose. Over cups of stewed tea in the hospital café they fell in love. Spoon was transformed. His new-found feelings made him generous and expansive, even happy. But when Rose herself became ill with the worry and the guilt, for the first time in his life, Spoon performed an unselfish act. Realizing that Rose would be happier without him despite their love, he packed his bags and left Jerusalem. Six months later he married Janet, a quiet girl from the records department in Halifax. Spoon had settled for a life of romantic disappointment.

It wasn't an ecstatic marriage, but a pleasant and decent one nevertheless, and when Janet passed away before her time, Spoon fell into a long, lonely period of sadness and self-pity. Six years went by, and when the grief subsided a little he found himself looking back across the years to the other love of his life. Now that his days were endless and empty he fell more and more to thinking about Rose. On a whim he drove to Jerusalem, saw that the house opposite was up for sale, and bought it.

The people of Jerusalem find that Spoon has mellowed over

time; maybe there is a cavity of charm and a chamber of warmth, trapped like air bubbles in that solid-steel heart. He's a subtle and sophisticated character, a smooth operator, a gentleman at times in his efforts to win over the hearts and minds of the local population, or the local electorate as they become. But there remains a darker, more sinister side to his personality. He is forceful and persuasive, always one step ahead, never appearing ruffled or wrong-footed. He's a man who looks like he can get whatever he wants, whenever he wants it, a man with a strange and powerful presence. Even the strongest begin to see things Spoon's way after half an hour or so in the man's company.

Six-foot-odd and powerfully built, Spoon is always well turned out in a worsted suit, white shirt, waistcoat and tie, complete with a fob-watch on a heavy gold chain. Habitually he produces the watch, flips the catch, notes the time and slips it back in his waistcoat pocket, all in one smooth action. He also enjoys a pinch of snuff, tipping the powder into a hollow at the base of his thumb before snorting it right to the back of his head, nostrils flaring, eyes open wide.

Rose Buckley was the prettiest girl in Jerusalem. She had her pick of husbands, and to this day she can't understand why she chose JE; he was a bully when she married him and hasn't altered much since. In those days she was an optimist, and thought she could bring to the fore the kind and caring man she could see somewhere inside him. But her early married years before the accident were a bitter let down. She grew to hate JE's regime of tyranny, and was on the point of leaving him when misfortune threw them together for ever.

Spoon's friendship and support became important – a lifeline. She could tell him how she really felt and he seemed to understand. To her surprise, delight and horror, she was falling in love. But Spoon left town on the early morning train, and after the birth of

her son, Wesley, she buckled down to life with JE. The husband
she'd come to despise was now totally dependent on her. She built
up a small business, flogging pet food and animal feedstuff to
families no less strange than her own. She'd found a measure of
independence, if it was only humping sacks of pony nuts and
cereal around the slippery pavements of Jerusalem.

Rose oversees an unsteady truce in the Castle home. She tries
to maintain the equilibrium of the house but her life is dominated
by JE's domestic needs. She manages a number of roles: wife,
nursemaid and housekeeper, and keeper of the peace between the
embittered JE and her son. Behind closed doors, family life at the
Castles' goes on under the foul-mouthed machine-gun invective
of JE's microphone, a contrast with the smooth tones of his 'public
announcement' voice.

Rose is knocked sideways when she looks out of the window
and sees Spoon letting himself into the house across the road. Not
only is she surprised to see him, but she's astonished by the feelings
she'd forgotten she had, feelings under lock and key, tidied away
in a box somewhere under the stairs, feelings that were never
meant to see the light of day again.

She's a good-looking woman, Rose, but without the time or
inclination to do anything about it. She puts on a bit of lipstick
to go out shopping. Once a month she treats herself to a perm,
coming home with a plastic rain-hood over her head, but two
hours later her hair is plastered to her head with running up and
down stairs, plumping her husband's pillows, wiping the sweat
from his brow and the foam from his mouth.

Wesley Castle is twenty-three and works for the Water Board.
Water is his element, and all of his spare time is spent fishing –
in the river, the canal, the reservoir – anywhere. He's reluctantly
joined the local volunteer fire service, with some heavy encouragement from his father. His lack of enthusiasm for the job and his

fear of the tasks involved have made for numerous humiliations and a handful of disciplinary proceedings, much to the shame and fury of his father, whose bravery and loyalty to the cause were legendary. Wesley just doesn't look the part: too much like his mum. The homo-erotic initiation ceremonies and endless practical jokes leave him ill at ease. He'd rather be fishing.

In every department Wesley is a failure, and JE is never slow to point out the differences between them. 'Call yourself a bloody fireman,' taunts JE through the tannoy, 'you couldn't put out a candle.' Wesley finds his tongue, answering back, even if it is on the floor below and out of earshot of the microphone. 'I'll murder that bastard, you see if I don't,' he says to himself one night, looking up from a textbook towards the bedroom above him. He's studying psychology at night-school, and he's just discovered Freud.

Slim, dark, potentially good-looking but not careful about his appearance, Wesley's wardrobe doesn't extend much beyond jeans, T-shirts and trainers, and an old leather jacket when he goes out. He wears glasses to read with. His hair could do with combing, or cutting, or both.

Softie is JE's link with the outside world, his eyes and his ears. He's a small man, wiry and self-contained. At times he appears subordinate and obedient, and seems to have no purpose other than maintaining the growing needs of JE. At other times he's content with his own company, a curious and likeable character, to be found in his workshop, tinkering with some new device, rattling through cryptic crosswords, entering every competition under the sun and quite often winning.

Five-foot-nothing and bald as a billiard ball, Softie is never happier than when he's up to his elbows in electrical cables or engine grease. The pockets of his NCB donkey jacket are stuffed with pliers, spanners, screwdrivers and the like.

Gert, JE's mother, lives next door. Through several years of being left to her own devices she's become eccentric in the extreme. Her house is full of fire-service memorabilia, inherited from her late husband, also a leading fireman. The house is populated with livestock, including geese and a donkey which roams freely from room to room. She's probably the only person able to exercise any degree of power over JE, and watching her, it isn't difficult to imagine where JE's vicious streak came from. 'Quack bloody quack,' she says to nobody in particular, filling in her bingo card as her son announces, 'Two little ducks, twenty-two,' on the radio. Rose avoids her like the plague; Wesley slides under her window-sill when he passes the house.

It's hard to say how old Gert is, exactly. She wears her hair piled up above her head, a flea-bitten fur coat at all times, and slips on a pair of seven-hole Doc Martens to go into town.

Wearing identical brown smocks, him with a pencil behind his ear and her with a roll of Sellotape for a bracelet, the Boots stand together behind the counter of their corner shop like Siamese twins, performing an age-old double act for their customers. Unlikely objects are bought, sold and bartered, including the most unappetizing organs of animals and birds. It reflects a sort of self-sufficiency and isolation that hangs over Jerusalem and its residents, like a bad smell that hasn't cleared. Their conversation never goes far beyond two practised responses. 'Thanking you,' says George Boot, handing over a slab of meat to a regular customer. 'Thanking you kindly indeed,' adds Edna Boot as she rings up the price on the till and holds out her hand for the money.

The Story So Far

While JE is observing the unloading of Spoon's van from the bedroom window, the telephone rings, and Alwin Wagstaff announces his retirement as Entertainments Secretary of Jerusalem Social Club at the end of the month. JE senses the opportunity of a lifetime. He could call out the bingo numbers over a public-address system wired from his bedroom, oversee events on closed-circuit television, and generally conduct proceedings from the comfort of his own home. The position would put him right back in the heart of Jerusalem, where he belongs, as well as bringing him the power and influence he craves and the respect he deserves. He switches on the transmitter to make known his intention to stand for election.

As he reaches the end of his address he sees Spoon locking his van and crossing the street to their house. 'Don't let that bastard in,' he bellows down the stairs, but it's too late. Rose is mortified and embarrassed by JE's rudeness, and by the confusion of her own feelings as Spoon steps gingerly across the threshold. 'I've come to see how you are . . . you know . . .' he says hesitatingly. 'I'm sorry, I'm just going out,' says Rose, hauling a sack of oatmeal over her back and setting off down the street.

JE broadcasts daily to the electorate of the social club, confident of victory. It looks like being a one-horse race – nobody wants to compete against a man confined to his bed through an act of historic bravery. 'You've got to take your hat off to a man like that. Poor bugger.'

Rose resists Spoon's attempts to get to know her again. She fears his reappearance could overturn the fragile balance in the Castle household.

Thwarted at Number 28, Spoon also finds it difficult to re-establish himself in the town. Everyone remembers Inspector

Spoon for different reasons; there are those who respect him and those who are frightened or suspicious. But he's determined to make a name for himself. When he finds out that JE is dragging his name through the mud on the airwaves, spreading gossip and lies, the germ of an idea begins to multiply. 'Kill a few birds with the one stone,' he mumbles to himself, as he fly-posts the first election poster of his campaign on the lamp-post opposite JE's window. Like Uncle Sam, Spoon's finger points from the picture, stretching out to the residents of Jerusalem above the date of the ballot: November 5th.

When JE hears of Spoon's plan to fight the election, he goes into orbit. He determines to drive Spoon out of town. The battle is drawn, nothing short of total annihilation will satisfy. As well as a public spectacle complete with manifestos, opinion polls, promises, persuasion, smear tactics, dirty tricks and bribery, the election campaign is a private and personal dog-fight between the two of them – a chance to settle old scores and to sort things out once and for all.

As the campaign hots up, JE makes full use of his ever-willing and undemonstrative side-kick, Softie, employing him to plaster the walls of the town with his picture, and leaflet or button-hole every member of the club. JE's tactic is to butter everyone up, and Softie has his work cut out for him, delivering fresh flowers and home-grown vegetables to all those identified as floating voters. JE's bedroom becomes a Campaign Head-quarters, with graphs on the wall charting public opinion, and JE addressing the electorate over the air, making impassioned speeches with *Jerusalem* or *Land of Hope and Glory* blaring in the background.

Spoon's campaigning is more targeted, more calculated. His house calls are short and sweet; quick, clean and clever, and almost always conclude with the promise of a vote. Everyone seems to owe Spoon a favour, and those that don't are the subjects of certain information – dossiers and photographs accumulated by Spoon during his police days, information that Spoon might be willing to let go or lose or forget about – for a price.

On his way back from a house call to an outlying voter, Spoon comes across Rose's van upside-down in a ditch, dog biscuits and birdseed scattered across the road. He shouts to Rose inside the car, and is distraught to receive no answer. He jumps down into the ditch and tries to wrench open the passenger door. He is crying, shouting, beating at the window with his fists. From across the road, bruised and dishevelled and half-hidden by a hedge, Rose watches in amazement. Her expression softens. As Spoon lifts a rock above his head to shatter the windscreen, she calls across to him. At that moment a vast flock of pigeons appears from nowhere, circles and swoops down to peck at the seeds. She smiles across at him. For the second time in their lives a near-fatal accident has drawn them together.

Slowly, delicately, their relationship rekindles. Rose is reluctant at first, but eventually Spoon becomes a regular if secret visitor to the house, drinking tea and eating butterfly cakes downstairs while JE bawls orders and requests from his bed in ignorance.

Rumours begin to circulate, just as they did all those years ago. They soon get to the ears of Wesley, in whose mind a terrible seed of doubt starts to grow. Counting backwards ... it couldn't be ... could it? He wouldn't dream of asking his mother, but his suspicions are further awakened when he returns early from work one day, finding Rose and Spoon sitting close together on the sofa. Rose tries to cover up: 'Mr Spoon was just showing me his flies.' And indeed it is true that Spoon has his fishing equipment, including his box of flies, with him in the room. To Wesley there can now be no doubt; a man who shares his passion for fishing and fly tying can surely be none other than his father.

Thrown into turmoil at first, Wesley slowly comes to terms with the idea, and is strangely relieved to think that JE might not be his dad. No need to try and fill the old man's boots any more; do your own thing, be your own man.

Wesley wants to find out more about Spoon. Early one morning he follows him to the canal and sets up twenty yards away. Spoon eyes him warily – is he about to be confronted about his feelings for Rose? Unsure how to strike up a conversation, Wesley lets his line drift downstream until his float becomes entangled with Spoon's; they begin to talk. There is a wise-owl quality to Spoon that emerges occasionally, a sort of guru-like presence. He explains to Wesley the paradox of fishing: namely, that the best fish lie in the deepest water, but to get anywhere near them means disturbing the surface, and so frightening away the fish. He equates this to life, saying that true peace is always invaded by the person who finds it, and therefore lost. He is full of such nuts of wisdom, and his ruminations appeal to Wesley's thoughtful and introspective nature. Their conversations on the tow-path become a regular thing.

From his vantage point in a bird-hide across the river, Softie witnesses these meetings and reports back to a hurt and furious J E. All his attempts to get any closer to his son end in disaster, the more so now that Wesley no longer feels the bonds of loyalty between them. On one occasion, J E summons Wesley to his bedroom in an effort to mend their differences and to do something fatherly. He hands Wesley a shoe box containing all of J E's fire-service medals and his own father's before him, telling Wesley that these are his inheritance, asking him to take care of them. Polished like the family silver, the medals gleam in the light. Embarrassed and uncomfortable, Wesley shuffles out of the bedroom leaving behind a bundle of books from Halifax library. J E begins inspecting the books, whose titles include *The Emergency Services – A Marxist Approach* and *Pump or Penis? Feminist Interpretations of Fire Fighting* edited by Angela Dabydeen. J E goes ballistic, cursing each one. Wesley walks out of the house as the books fly from the bedroom window and crash down around him in the street.

In quieter moments, JE sits in his blankets running Super 8 cine films against the bedroom wall. He watches flickering images of Rose as his beautiful young wife, laughing and throwing snowballs in the park, then scenes of Wesley as a child, on the beach, building sand-castles and eating ice-cream. Wesley runs towards the camera and turns it on JE, hunched in his wheelchair, trying to cover the lens with his hand. As the film streams past, JE gazes at the wall, silently, tears rolling down his cheeks.

As the campaign continues, Spoon coerces the Boots into his camp by suggesting they might not relish a visit from the health and hygiene people, and by threatening to reveal their illegal offal-smuggling business. 'Thanking you ... Thanking you kindly indeed,' say the Boots as they slide a packet of sausages across the counter to Spoon. Back home Spoon takes one sniff of the sausages and tosses them into the bin.

Alwin Wagstaff, the outgoing Entertainments Secretary, is supposed to remain neutral in his overseeing of the election, but his relationship with Gert, JE's mother, calls his objectivity into question. He has been seen on a number of occasions leaving her house late at night by the back door, often dishevelled and flustered, and on one evening wearing what appeared to be a studded dog-collar and handcuffs.

A public debate is held between the two candidates, at the club. JE attends in the shape and form of a television, loudspeaker and microphone contraption, rigged up and operated by the diligent and dextrous Softie. At the other end of the platform, Spoon is smartly dressed, well informed, and charming.

[*A packed house at Jerusalem Social Club, all seats taken. ALWIN WAGSTAFF is centre-stage, dressed in a dicky-bow and tuxedo, puffing on an enormous cigar. To his right, SPOON stands behind a lectern with his arms crossed in front of him, impeccably groomed, dressed in a dark suit and tie. To WAGSTAFF's left, an ancient television encased in a mahogany cabinet flickers on top of two in-turned chairs, with a loudspeaker at either side and a microphone craning over the top towards the audience.]*

WAGSTAFF *[clearing his throat]*: Ladies and gentlemen, best of order if you please. We all know why we're here, so let's get on with it. I'm sure neither candidate needs introducing, but I'll introduce them in any case, beginning with Mr Spoon on my right.

SPOON: Good evening.

WAGSTAFF: And on my left, er, in spirit if not in body, Mr John Edward Castle. Can you hear me, JE?

[Silence. The TV continues to flicker.]

WAGSTAFF: JE, can you hear me?

NEVILLE SHACKLETON *[from the back of the hall, with a pint in his hand]*: Ground control to Major Tom.

[Much laughter in the hall.]

WAGSTAFF: Best of order, please.

NEVILLE SHACKLETON: Is there anybody out there?

DONALD STONEWOOD *[also from the back of the hall, also with a pint in his hand]*: One small step for man, one giant leap for mankind.

[The back of the hall erupts with laughter.]

WAGSTAFF: Best of order, please. Can anybody sort this thing out?

[SOFTIE leaps on to the stage from his seat in the front row, and begins adjusting the horizontal hold on the television until a picture

of JE's face emerges, obviously in the bedroom of his house, spruced up and with his hair slicked back, wearing a patch of tissue on a shaving cut and adjusting his tie.]

SOFTIE: We've started, JE. Lift off. You're on the air.

JE *[ruffled, and looking down at his notes]*: Oh, er, er, good evening everybody. *[He continues, reading from a script.]* Friends, family and acquaintances, I'd like to begin by thanking you for giving up your valuable time this evening to come and see things as they really are.

WAGSTAFF: Yes, thanks JE. Now, if I could . . .

JE: *[cutting across him]*: It's my opinion, and one which I share with all right-minded people of this town, that the position of Entertainments Secretary is a position of honour and responsibility . . .

WAGSTAFF: Thank you, JE. I really do feel that we should be . . .

JE *[carrying on regardless]*: And with this in mind I've put my own name forward, as a man who's lived and breathed Jerusalem since the day he was born, and not some fly-by-night, here one minute and gone the next . . .

[Wesley slides down in his seat. Rose covers her face with her hand.]

WAGSTAFF: JE, I really think we should . . .

GERT *[intervening]*: Oh shut up, for God's sake, JE, or we'll be here till bloody midnight.

[JE becomes silent.]

ROSE *[to Wesley]*: I can't bear it. I'm going.

WESLEY *[taking hold of her hand and pulling her back into her seat]*: Come on, Mum. Give him a chance.

WAGSTAFF: Thank you, JE. And thank you, Gert.

[GERT winks at WAGSTAFF, who blushes and almost loses his cigar.]

WAGSTAFF: Without further ado, then, does anyone have any questions?

[Almost everyone in the hall raises an arm. WAGSTAFF picks out COLIN BUTTERWORTH at the back.]

COLIN BUTTERWORTH *[being egged on by his pals]*: Wor about doffers?

WAGSTAFF: I beg your pardon?

COLIN BUTTERWORTH: Wor about doffers? Strippers?

WAGSTAFF: What about them?

COLIN BUTTERWORTH: Well, will we have 'em, or won't we?

WAGSTAFF: I see. I'll put that question to Mr Castle first. JE, as I understand it the question is as follows: should you be elected, would you be inviting strippers to come and . . . er . . . perform at the club?

JE: Well, as far as I'm concerned it's just a bit of harmless fun, isn't it?

[Someone at the back shouts 'speak up a bit'. SOFTIE stands up and adjusts a knob connected to the TV by a long length of cable. The word 'volume' appears across JE's face, along with a set of red dots that increase from left to right.]

JE: Always has been, always will.

NOREEN KNOWLES *[standing up in the middle of the hall, shouting]*: It's a disgrace.

[Lots of agreement amongst the women.]

JE *[flustered, trying to keep on top of the situation]*: It's not something I'd be interested in personally, obviously, but it's traditional, isn't it? And if somebody wants to get their kit off on stage, she can do, and those who want to watch can watch, and those who don't want to don't have to. Yes. Thank you.

ROSE *[under her breath]*: Nude women? He'd run a mile.

WESLEY: Aye, if he could.

[ROSE slaps WESLEY on the knee but has to smile at the same time.]

NOREEN KNOWLES *[standing again]*: It's a disgrace, that's what I say.

PAULINE MUMP: I agree.

WAGSTAFF: Thank you everybody. Best of order, please.

COLIN BUTTERWORTH: Wor about you, Spoon? Are we goin' to have strippers or not?

SPOON *[taking his time]*: Male or female, Mr Butterworth? Which are you interested in?

[There is a great roar of laughter, especially from the back of the hall. COLIN BUTTERWORTH goes red and sits down.]

SPOON *[self-assured, speaking clearly and confidently]*: In my view, it's the feeling of the membership that counts, not just the opinion of one man. After all, we don't want to hurt anybody's feelings. But I will say this: Jerusalem Social Club has a reputation second to none, and a waiting list that reflects that reputation. I should also say that we shouldn't ask anyone to do anything that we wouldn't be prepared to do ourselves, so I suggest we think long and hard about this one, unless of course Mr Butterworth wants to come up here and show us what he had in mind.

[Uproar and cheers in the hall. There is general agreement, and a lot of nodding of heads.]

WAGSTAFF: Lewis Pike, your question please.

LEWIS PIKE *[standing, and reading from the back of an envelope]*: I'd like to ask Mr Spoon and Mr Castle about their qualifications for the job, relevant experience and so on, and the sorts of entertainment we can expect to see at the club, bearing in mind the excellent standard set by Mr Wagstaff over previous years.

WAGSTAFF: Very kind of you to say so, Lewis. Very kind.

LEWIS PIKE *[standing again to reply]*: Pleasure, Alwin.

WAGSTAFF: Mr Spoon?

SPOON: During the years I've been away from Jerusalem, I built up a successful chauffeur and escort service – looking after some very big names, making arrangements for tours, hospitality and such like, and I can tell you that I made some very important contacts along the way. As proof of this, I'd like to offer this letter, just as a taste of things to come.

[SPOON takes a letter from his inside breast pocket, and hands it to WAGSTAFF. WAGSTAFF puts on his glasses, unfolds the letter and reads from it.]

WAGSTAFF: 'My dear Mr Spoon. Just a short note to thank you for all your endless patience and dedicated professionalism, and for making my tour a very smooth and successful one. If I can ever repay the favour, please don't hesitate to ask. Yours affectionately, Shirley . . .' *[to SPOON]*: I can't quite make out the signature.

SPOON: Bassey, I think you'll find. Shirley Bassey.

[Uproar again in the hall. Lots of excitement.]

SPOON *[producing a whole wad of letters bound in a red ribbon]*: And there are plenty more where that came from.

GERT *[standing up]*: It's bollocks. Tell him, John.

JE *[gob-smacked]*: I don't believe it.

WAGSTAFF *[smelling the letter]*: Perfumed as well.

[ROSE bites her lip, hiding her feelings.]

WESLEY *[to himself]*: Unbelievable.

GERT: It's rubbish. All rubbish. Tell him, John.

JE [*complying with his mother's instruction, losing his cool*]: Oh very smart, Spoon, very smart. But don't think we don't know what's going on. Don't think we can't see right through you. You think you can come here with your fancy talk and fancy letters, and pull the wool over everybody's eyes, don't you?

WESLEY [*to himself*]: Here we go.

[*JE bangs the camera with his head, and carries on talking with only half of his face in frame.*]

JE: Well let me tell you, you've got it wrong. All wrong. This isn't the London Palladium, and I don't care if you've got promises from Elvis Presley or Jesus bloody Christ for that matter, because they're not needed.

ROSE [*standing up*]: John, will you calm down? You'll make yourself poorly.

GERT: Let him talk, woman.

JE: Tradition, that's what this club's built on. Bingo Friday and Saturday night, a singer or comic from Leeds or Bradford, Manchester even every now and again, the odd Country and Western night, discos, race trips, raffles, a bit of supper . . . It's that kind of thing that makes this club what it is, and that's what people want. Am I right, everybody? You tell him, you tell him that's what you want.

[*There is silence in the hall.*]

NOREEN KNOWLES [*standing, to* SPOON]: Have you really met Shirley Bassey?

SPOON: Well, I . . .

JE [*irate now, out of breath and in a real lather*]: Has he bloody hell as like. And what do we care if he has? What do we care if he's met Shirley MacLaine or Shirley bloody Williams. We don't need 'em. Shirley Bassey my arse. Who's he going to bring up next? Tom Jones?

SPOON: Actually, it's funny that you should mention Tom, because it was only last week . . .

[*There is a crackle of electricity and JE's TV goes dead.*]

NOREEN KNOWLES: If he can get Tom Jones, he's good enough for me!

[*The club erupts again at the prospect of Tom Jones. GERT gets up from her seat in a fury.*]

GERT: Have you no respect? For a man who gave the best years of his life and both his legs for this town?

[*Shouts of 'Sit down, you old bat.' GERT throws her pint tankard towards the direction of the shout. Chaos breaks out. Another glass flies towards the front of the room. WAGSTAFF bangs his gavel.*]

There is almost a riot in the hall. Rose turns on Spoon and snaps at him for belittling JE in public, then runs home to her husband to save him from embarrassing her and humiliating himself further. Spoon follows her back to the house, and arriving there finds the door open but no answer. He can hear voices so he goes inside, to the kitchen, and over the tannoy he hears Rose and JE upstairs, JE hysterical with rage. JE rants on about Spoon, accusing Rose of unfaithfulness all those years ago. Evidently it is an argument they have rehearsed many, many times over; the cadences of Rose's weary protests sound as well-worn as JE's raving accusations. Eventually JE's anger turns to tears. Rose tries to comfort him. Spoon sits in the kitchen, downstairs, listening to JE demoralized and sobbing, and Rose's voice whispering, 'There, there, it's all right now, come on, it'll be all right.'

Bonfire Night – the night of the election. The whole of Jerusalem is illuminated with the biggest bonfire imaginable and alive with the snap, crackle and pop of fireworks. Members drift into the club all evening to cast their votes, and are greeted on the doorstep by Spoon, who gives everyone a very firm handshake and a straight look. At the other end of town, Wesley attends a fire at an old farmhouse. Fire crackles inside, smoke pours out of every window, and it looks as if the roof is about to collapse. Wesley puts on the breathing equipment with instructions to go in. Terrified, he enters the house with the blaze reflecting on his visor and images of JE's accident flashing in front of his eyes. Rigid with fear, a trickle of urine runs out over his boots. Just when it looks as if he might faint he is pulled out of the fire by a colleague. Spitting with venom and calling him a chicken-shit coward, the chief-officer punches him in the face, calls him a disgrace to the uniform and sends him home.

Back in bed, JE goes wild when Wesley brings him the news, telling him he has brought shame on the family. Their full-scale war of words culminates in Wesley tearing the tannoy from the mantelpiece, throwing it into a cupboard and slamming the door, JE's voice still raging like a man trapped in a coffin. JE, or rather the tannoy, is rescued by Rose, as Wesley storms out of the house and into the pub.

Rose leaves the house to go and cast her vote, and meets Spoon standing on the steps of the club. Rose becomes tearful, telling him she doesn't know what to do for the best. Spoon puts his arm around her, tells her to follow her heart. A rocket goes up into the sky and explodes, lighting them for a split second like the flash of a camera.

Towards the end of the evening, Spoon goes into the club and asks 'which way the wind is blowing'. Elsie Conroy, speaking out of turn, tells him that as things stand the election is a dead heat, with only himself and Wesley still to vote. Spoon goes back on to the steps and lights a cigarette.

Suddenly, Wesley arrives in a drunken rage, cursing JE, saying that he'll vote against him, out of sheer spite. 'That'll show the old bastard, won't it?' On the other hand, if he lost, life in the Castle house wouldn't be worth living – especially for his mother. Spoon tells him not to be too hard on JE – it can't be easy being cooped up in a bedroom all day. Can't be easy, trying to be a father in that state. Plucking up courage, Wesley asks, 'Ever have children yourself, then?'

'No,' replies Spoon. 'Plumbing problem.'

Spoon tells Wesley that it's too late to vote, because the poll is closed. Demoralized and defeated in every way, Wesley wanders off into the night, a loser once again, and a failure. Spoon extinguishes his cigarette by grinding it into the ground, goes into the club and casts the final vote.

Elsie Conroy picks up the telephone. We follow the cable underground, then up and over and across the houses and telegraph poles of Jerusalem and in through the bedroom window of the Castle house. The telephone rings. Elsie Conroy informs JE that by the margin of a single vote he is the new Entertainments Secretary of Jerusalem Social Club. It's official. JE goes straight to his broadcasting equipment and begins transmitting the news. He is jubilant, triumphant, ecstatic, victorious, unbearable. He delivers a pre-prepared acceptance speech full of excessive promises and thanks to all his loyal supporters. He even manages, magnanimously, to find a kind word for his beaten opponent, Spoon, but speculates that a man with any pride would have to leave town with his tail between his legs after such a humiliating defeat.

His broadcast continues over the following scenes.

Gert leans towards the bedside table, turns on the radio and listens to her son proclaiming the good news. She lifts a pint of tea from the Teasmade and settles herself in bed. On the pillow next to her are a pair of feet. At the bottom end of the bed, Alwin Wagstaff's face emerges. He hears the result, looks around the room and pulls the covers back over his face.

The Boots stand behind the counter of their shop as they listen to JE's voice on the radio. Mr Boot crosses himself as he hears the result. 'Thanking you, Mrs Boot.' 'Thanking you kindly indeed, Mr Boot.' Mrs Boot bends to the pile of newspapers and kindling in the hearth and puts a light to it. Outside, a plume of white smoke rises from the chimney.

In the second-hand-car showroom, Spoon's van sits under a handwritten sign: 'Bargain of the week. One careful owner.' In Spoon's back garden, a pile of furniture and clothes is burning in a small bonfire, unattended.

Bleepers go off in the homes of several volunteer firemen, and the telephone rings in the snug of the Hare and Hounds. Firemen race towards the station and fling open the doors, only to find the fire-engine vanished into thin air. They stand around, scratching their heads.

Somewhere on the shore of a Scottish loch in the early morning mist we discover the said fire-engine, its turntable ladder fully extended out over the lake, with Wesley sat on the last rung, fishing from the deepest water, undisturbed. He hauls out another trout and drops it into the bucket which swings from the ladder.

Softie walks down Jerusalem's main street, tearing down the election posters and ramming the shredded paper into a bin bag.

As JE's speech soars, we see Spoon walking out on to the empty platform of Jerusalem railway station with his suitcase, wearing the same clothes he arrived in. He takes a pinch of snuff. He checks his fob-watch, and with one fluent movement slips it back in his pocket. A minute later, Rose emerges behind him on the platform, also carrying a suitcase. They stand about ten feet apart, aware of each other's presence, but not acknowledging it. The train arrives, obscuring our view from the other side of the line, and when it pulls out the platform is empty.

J E's commentary has now reached the heights of a church sermon. Looking out over the town, the remains of the bonfire are still smouldering in the valley bottom as the train disappears into the tunnel.

THE END

Sport in the Region

Over to see Craig, who's moved to Sheffield. We walk down to Hillsborough to see if we can get into the semi-final, either by paying on the turnstile or buying a ticket outside the ground. We're instantly recognizable as neutrals as we mill about outside the main gate, because we're the only ones not wearing a red and white clown wig (Middlesbrough) or blue and white face-paint (Chesterfield). We do three laps of the stadium and only meet one tout, a fat boy sat on a garden wall who wants a hundred quid for two thirty-pound tickets. When we tell him we won't bother, he says, 'I don't blame you. The bottom's really fallen out of this racket. There's another lad up there with a few left but he's a bit dodgy. You're better off watching it in the pub for free. Have a few pints.'

In the Travellers, there are about fifty people sitting around the big screen, half of them smoking dope, the other half eating a pile of sandwiches. Three coppers are looking in through the window, watching the game. When Middlesbrough go two up, someone throws a chip buttie at Ravanelli, and he celebrates with his shirt over his head and tomato sauce splattered against the outline of his face. Sky keeps flashing up the scores from other matches. Sheffield Wednesday are losing four-nil at Blackburn, which doesn't help matters. After the game, the man who threw the sandwich goes into the beer garden with two of his mates, and smashes one of the wooden tables. Armed with lengths of 4 × 2, they wait for the Middlesbrough fans who've left their cars in the pub car park, and we have to walk through them, heads down, past the policemen who don't want to know. You've got a black eye at the moment, and you're not sure if this makes you less of a target ('Leave him alone, poor bugger') or more ('He's had some already so he won't mind it again'). We walk back to the house to watch the highlights on *Match of the Day – the Road to Wembley*. The BBC. Des Lynam.

Craig's brother-in-law phones up to tell Craig he's an uncle. Erin. 6 lbs 9 oz. It's either Tequila or Bailey's Irish Cream to celebrate, and in the end it's both at once, with bacon and egg to finish with. Craig's been in the studio recording a couple of songs. He plays them through on the stereo, and you tell him it sounds like one of those Scottish bands from the eighties, like Orange Juice or Aztec Camera or Josef K. He says, 'No, you're wrong. It's the sound of young Huddersfield.'

Results Just In, Plus Details of a Forthcoming Fixture

Most things have been settled this week. United are out of the European Cup, but should win the league if they hold their nerve and Arsenal and Liverpool keep losing theirs. Town have addled the three points they needed to be sure of avoiding the drop, scraping home 2–1 against Southend in front of a four-and-a-half-thousand crowd. And Barnsley are in the Premiership. The *Observer* wonders how many times cobbles, pits, flat caps and Dickie Bird will be mentioned between now and their first match next season, under the headline *By'eck . . . Dickie Bird's in tears as the boys from Barnsley join the Big League.*

This only leaves the small matter of the general election to be sorted out, and in an unusual burst of political conscientiousness, you've been leafing through some of the electoral junk-mail to fall through the letterbox these past few days – glossy, personalized brochures, promising the earth. What's so striking about them is that with their headlines and bullet points and underlinings and capital letters, they take the form of an advert, and therefore provoke in the reader an instant sensation of being 'had'. You conclude from this that the people putting them together must think that us lot here in votesville are totally stupid. Worse still, if it works, they must be right. Having said that, if the apparent importance of deciding who to vote for can be overlooked for a moment, it's possible to see further into these leaflets – like staring into one of those magic-eye pictures – and suddenly something superbly entertaining comes into view. They're fantastic, and even if the flyer for the Tory, Graham Riddick, is no more fantastic than the others, it's a compelling read. Not only that, but after eighteen years of the same government, a lifetime of only ever voting on the losing side in a general election, and on the eve of the country finally looking as if it might do something about it – it's asking for it.

Riddick, a blond-haired, blue-eyed boy with a chin you could walk a dog on, was involved in the early rounds of the cash-for-questions kerfuffle. He's very much the Anglo-Saxon candidate in this constituency, and appears on the front cover of his four-page, gatefold A4 proclamation as the family man, perched on a comfy, floral-patterned chair with his wife and three children, all nestled within his outstretched arms. A woollen jumper (M&S?) speaks of a semi-rural, local homeliness. On a ledge behind him, an old black-and-white photograph of an important-looking man with tie, moustache and greased-back hair says something about heritage, tradition, birthright and history. On a window-sill sits a shiny new toy in the shape of a crash helmet, suggesting Dad on his knees with the kids, making time for family life despite the crushing schedule of the modern constituency MP. You can imagine the hand of the official photographer, selecting and placing the crucial objects within his field of vision. You can hear the precarious silence of a staged composition, holding its breath before the shutter clicks. Big smiles. Cheese.

In blue upper-case letters, PLEASE CIRCULATE THIS LEAFLET WITHIN YOUR HOUSEHOLD. Honestly. Followed by 'A Personal Message from Graham Riddick,' with a photocopied signature. Or is that an autograph? Either way, we're flattered. We're honoured. Coyly, he gives his place of residence as 'between Holmfirth and Penistone', not so much an address or even a location, but a vector of several miles in length, inferring that a) The sitting MP for Colne Valley lives in a surrealist universe where the constructs of place and direction have become transposed, or b) The woolly jumper is actually a tantalizing reference to Riddick's secret life as a New Age Traveller, existing along what might be a powerful ley-line, or c) Graham Riddick does not want to be bothered at home. Those people considering invading his privacy, wherever it happens to be, should be warned that he lists shooting as one of his hobbies, which in the light of the Dunblane massacre and the debate that followed is a fairly flabbergasting thing to be boasting about in an election campaign. And like most people who dabble with guns, Riddick is very hot on law and order. In bold type, he supports 'Corporal punishment for juvenile offenders and capital punishment for murderers.'

Across the centre spread of the leaflet are several colour photographs, the best of which is Graham Riddick on the bottom edge of Marsden golf-course, under Pule Hill. In a suit and tie, visible from the waist up, he stands in an area of out-of-bounds – the bus turn-around below the first fairway – and leans comfortably with his left hand against a wire fence (barbed? electric?). Behind him, a man in a green jacket could be walking his dog, looking for a lost ball, or carrying out his duties as a plain-clothes security guard, checking for assassins and booby traps in the rough below the ladies' tee. It seems petulant to notice such details, rude even, but it's irresistible. There's a derelict farmhouse in the background, just auctioned for seventy-odd thousand after squatters moved out and the roof slates were filched by a gang of builders from Lancashire. The fence that Riddick leans against might well be part of Marsden's complex Sheep Control Scheme, Colne Valley's version of the Australian Dingo Barrier, culminating in a cattle grid at the top of Old Mount Road with a gate to one side, so badly fitted that the sheep crawl underneath it. There are no leaves on the trees, but on an unusually calm day on the wintry summit of the Pennines there isn't enough breeze to lift the flaxen wing of Mr Riddick's home-cropped fringe. A hazard-warning post on the golf-course stands out above his right shoulder.

Looking for too long at the blue lettering, you remember a couple of weeks ago seeing a farmer putting up Tory signs along the edge of his field, next to the road between Honley and Meltham. He was standing on the back of his trailer, driving a stake into the ground, bringing a sledge-hammer down on to the word Riddick. Cynicism can help, but in the end, only irony can save us from becoming the people they want us to be.

A Casting Vote

Ten a.m. to the dentist, then to see Gran in the old folks' flats, down by the river. The old village stocks are near the entrance – bleached wood and rusty chains, displayed in a semi-circular stone wall. 'Corporal punishment for juvenile offenders, capital punishment for murderers.' There's a pile of grit left over from winter with a crust of salt catching the sunlight.

It's warm.

Inside the flats, it's even warmer, a steady seventy-odd degrees to stop any of the residents seizing up. Gran asks why you're 'talking funny', and when you tell her you've been for a crown fitting, she says, 'Why, what have you won this time?'

It's a gold crown. Well, gold in the way that a ten-pence-piece is silver, and like any foreign object in the mouth, it feels like Sugar Loaf Mountain, or the Rock of Gibraltar. But it's gloriously smooth, and you can't stop stroking your tongue against it, feeling for the rough peg of the old tooth like a rusty nail, finding a nugget of precious metal in its place. It's a pharaoh's tooth. What do the Germans say? 'The early morning has gold in its mouth.' A good way of getting married – a gold tooth instead of a ring. All the connotations, all the consequences.

You park in the playground and go into your old junior school under the word GIRLS carved into the stone above the door. There's something lavatorial about voting, doing what you have to do with your back to the world, in a cubicle, fiddling around at waist height then walking over to the basin or hand-dryer of the ballot box. At least, if you're a man there is. Quiet as well, the same sort of hush, or odd remarks relating to anything other than the reason for being there, like in a doctor's waiting-room.

Looking at the slip of paper, it suddenly crosses your mind to do the wrong thing, the other thing, just to see what it feels like, just for that one moment of perversion. One vote can't make any difference, can it? A lot of people do it – is it like a little electric shock of pleasure or pain, or something more sensational? The pen hovers over the paper, and you think of that split second in the dentist's chair, when the drill comes tearing into the little hidy-hole of flesh where the nerve is cowering, the nerve that connects the toes and fingertips and testicles with a burst of several thousand smouldering volts of alternating current carried on razor-wire. That moment.

The other thing about voting is that it's secret. Anonymous. Tell anyone, and it won't come true. It's like making a wish or keeping your fingers crossed or saying a prayer before going to bed. It's like putting a tooth under the pillow, and waiting for morning.

Albert Victor Forgets Himself

And their eyes were opened and they knew him; and he vanished out of their sight. Luke xxiv.31

Introducing Albert Victor Grayson,
something of a mystery.
September 1920, history remembers
he was lodging in a plush apartment
in a well-to-do vicinity:
the parish of St James' Palace,
Bury Street, suite forty-two,
located on the fourth floor, with a view
and half a dozen hand-picked neighbours.

Lunch-time, when a pair of strangers
visited his rooms, sent up a card,
sent out for drinks and drank all afternoon,
descended in the lift
and called a taxi.

Minutes later, with his luggage,
Albert Victor followed suit, and left.

Upon investigation, Grayson's rooms were found
devoid of personal effects.
What follows is a combination
of detection, recollection, figures, facts, and speculation.

Let it be a lesson:
Grayson, Albert Victor, in Memoriam
from 1881
to God knows where and God knows when.

Albert Victor Grayson was a sensation. From nowhere and nothing, he shot to fame in a dramatic by-election in 1907 in Colne Valley – the first socialist ever to represent the constituency. He was dubbed as the greatest orator of his day, and tipped as a future leader of the Labour Party. He took his seat in the Commons, but fell foul of his colleagues by ignoring the tradition that maiden speeches in the House should be uncontroversial. Instead of ingratiating himself, he lambasted the Government for awarding a £50,000 fat-cat pension to Lord Cromer in recognition of his services in Egypt. In his next parliamentary performance, Grayson interrupted a debate of the Licensing Bill to voice his support for the unemployed, his contempt for the government, and his opinion of his fellow-socialists as class traitors. After eleven further interruptions, he was suspended from the House, and left the Chamber shouting, 'This is a House of Murderers.' Grayson was young and good looking. He was a lady's man, but not exclusively, according to a letter to his friend Harry Dawson, unless a profound desire to lick the epidermis of a friend is political morse code between two revolutionary socialists. He liked the high life and he liked a drink, liked them to the extent that his attendance record in the Commons was abysmal. He lost his seat at the next election, and for the next ten years made occasional attempts to resurrect his political career, breaking off to fight a war in between.

Then in 1920, Grayson walked out of his lodgings in London, and was never seen again. Despite reported sightings from as far away as Spain and New Zealand, Grayson had officially vanished from the surface of the earth. As a disappearing act, it made John Stonehouse's effort fifty-odd years later look like a game of hide and seek, and Grayson never returned from that strange place where Lord Lucan sits down to tea with Donald Crowhurst, and Elvis and Glenn Miller dream up a joint come-back album.

In 1921, an entry in the college records read
that Albert Victor Grayson, former undergraduate, was dead.
The next report in 1924, from Maidstone, Kent,
where I turned up for some political event
and indicated to a man called Cox
just who I was.
I had the face of a man in shock.
Next, I was dead again according to some Yorkshire quack,
then well again and spotted upstairs on a double-decker bus
near Charing Cross,
then seen in Southern France
consorting with a rich man's wife in 1929,
then working in a London shop,
then ten years later I was riding on the District Line,
well-heeled, in morning dress and topper looking firm and
    fit,
escorted by a lady who referred to me as 'Vic',
then struck down in the Blitz,
then buried in Australia,
then supping in a Herne Bay public bar,
then sending notes to relatives in Canada.
And not one for the quiet life
I surfaced then in Tyneside
having changed my name to Wilson, John, and married.
Then recognized by speedway ace Rex Ranby in Madrid
who said that when he collared me I looked electrified.
Then signing for my medals at the Ministry in 1939,

and finally, aged seventy-five, obese
with swollen legs, no teeth,
living alone in King's Cross Road,
whiling away the last of the long days
when my monogrammed cuff-links gave me away.
Allegedly.
Not bad going for the life and times
of a man supposedly out of sight and out of mind.

During his victorious campaign of 1907, Grayson turned up in Marsden to blurt out his policies from the back of a cart and to win the hearts and minds of the locals. Isobel Armitage, a schoolgirl at the time, remembers the pretty twenty-five-year-old running his fingers through his hair and smirking at the women before launching into his fiery message of uprising and revolt. As a mill-owner's daughter she wasn't impressed. When Grayson was announced the winner, mobs ran through the streets singing *Jerusalem*, carrying the red flag, and she thought that her father would be attacked and killed. Isobel died this year, leaving a big house in the village in need of considerable attention and an asbestos problem in one of the wings.

Mysteries tend to become more mysterious. Grayson's upbringing and education from such unlikely beginnings was always something of a puzzle. Rumours of a private benefactor, coupled with Grayson's aristocratic facial features, plus the choice of Albert Victor as a name, all led to speculations of a royal kind. And when on her deathbed his mother was reported to have called out 'the Marlboroughs, the Marlboroughs', it was taken as more than a final request for a favourite brand of cigarette. Then there's also the riddle of the missing library book, *Victor Grayson – Labour's Lost Leader* by David Clark, borrowed from Huddersfield Lending Library on 9th August 1994, and never returned. Records indicate a subscriber in the Marsden area as the likely culprit, and until the book passes across the barcode scanner of that establishment and finds its way back to shelving area 329.942 092, all lending services to that member will be withdrawn.

It's a pretty good read considering it's the biography of someone who covered his tracks completely, and that it's written by a man who was a Labour MP for Colne Valley himself, and therefore 'involved'. But the most moving part is the series of photographs stitched into the middle, showing Grayson in a variety of moods and circumstances. It's odd to be staring into the face of a man before he absented himself from the known world, odd to be looking for the danger signs, the warnings, the clues. Ironic as well. Grayson was famous before the mass reproduction and circulation of photographic film, which meant that hardly anyone recognized him, which of course made it easier to slip away. Staring into these snaps now is a trick of the light, a form of wisdom after the event. But they came too late in the search for a man who on his last birthday would have been one hundred and sixteen. Neither do any recordings of Grayson's voice exist. So in the BBC Radio 3 programme produced by Fiona MacLean in 1995, it took an actor to make a guess at the man's apparently accentless English, and a third party to put words in his mouth.

Some images in black and white, in retrospect.
The first, me standing
on a set of wooden steps
in front of windows and a balcony.
Me smartly dressed:
a decent single-breasted suit – if slightly crumpled
at the sleeves, and creased from sitting,
just above the knees.
Hair parted on the right – your right, my left –
swept back with oil or cream or grease
except for one stray lock,

161

a second hand at twenty-five-to, stopped
against a confident but weary face.
Two alabaster hands, one hanging at the waist,
the other resting on an iron rail.
And that expression – frown, or smile.

A second snap, soft focus,
head and shoulders.
Stiff wing-collar, boil-washed, starched
and sat up straight.
Black tie, precisely knotted, loosened though
and lowered, not too tight,
then tucked behind a waistcoat buttoned to the top,
topped with a matching jacket in a decent cloth,
well cut, a herringbone perhaps. Hard wearing.
Wonderfully groomed,
except a button-hole without a bloom.
Eyes forward, dark,
each pin-pricked with a point of light.
Clean-shaven, boyish, fresh, unruffled, clean,
untroubled, knowing, healthy, lean.
The rest off-camera, trimmed to fit the frame,
the head off-centre, just by two or three degrees.
Tight-lipped and silent. Watch the birdie, Vic. Say cheese.

The third, a close-up at a desk
with some illuminated text.
In better light I see that suit is tweed.
This is a pose, a bluff, a lie:
the index finger of the left hand
notes a word or line,
the right hand holds a pencil to the page
and writes.
A magnifying glass, face down,

expands the thing it sees.
Mid-sentence, penning some important speech?
I think not.
Look, a lily in the background cranes its neck
to get in shot.

The fourth, me at the old joanna,
some plain upright thing,
not grand,
with blurred, untellable sheet music
open on the stand.
Soft pedal, bottom hand.

The fifth, me in the garden leaning on the mower –
strange contraption that
consisting of a cutter and a roller.
Trellis, pergola and arbour, border, clover. Summer.

Sixth, a panorama almost – Scapegoat Hill.
Me in the thick of it,
a dapper and polite pied piper,
out in front before a crocodile of voters
to declare a Labour Club
in my constituency well and truly open.
Out behind, a line of people from the valley
stretching back a mile or so, unbroken.
Cane, hat, trilby, and a button-hole,
a red carnation
if I'm not mistaken.

All Points North

Then to this.
A dimple to the chin, a pin-stripe to the suit,
a pocket watch beneath the breast.
A knowingness. A certainty.
The last surviving print. The state of me.
It's winter, judging by the nature of the trees.

News Just In

The *Independent on Sunday*, 27th April. Sue Gaisford: 'Finally, it would be criminal of me not to mention the recent gripping events in *The Archers* (R4). Vanessa Whitburn has done it again. Everywhere I go, the talk is of how Simon Armitage should be punished for his violent attack on the innocent Debbie. For once, it's not the saintly Shula who is the victim, though she should certainly have warned her cousin, we now know. Anna Ford is at last thoroughly vindicated for calling him a shit. My dentist thinks he should be castrated.'

News Just In

The *Independent on Sunday*, 4th May. Sue Gaisford: 'And talking of how we deceive ourselves, by some extraordinary trick of the light, last week's column suggested that the charming and gifted poet Simon Armitage, presenter of R4's prestigious *Stanza* series, has strayed into Ambridge and started to wreak havoc. It's not true. It was, of course, Simon Pemberton who has earned the wrath of the nation. I must have my eyes tested.'

Sport in the Region

Eric Cantona is dead. You were trying to tune in a new telly the other day, and at the point when you'd got a half-decent picture but no sound, you saw a small crowd weeping outside Old Trafford, the sight of a mournful-looking Alex Ferguson shrugging his shoulders and shaking his head, and a slow-motion, soft-focus sequence of Eric in action, including some of his miracles and a couple of his atrocities. Alex was wearing that sleeping-bag coat, the one he wears on the touchline. A sickly looking Jordi Cruyff was saying something heartfelt – Jordi Cruyff, who was spotted in IKEA at Christmas, quite wisely investing in furniture that can be easily disassembled and transported. You then watch footage of the Subbuteo-sized Juninho running through the legs of Tony Adams, stood there like the Colossus of Rhodes, and consider it bad taste that the press should be sizing up Cantona's replacement with the Frenchman still warm on the slab.

As it turns out, when sound unites with vision, Eric has hung up his boots, and is thinking of turning his mind to matters of a higher order, such as poetry. You wonder how long he'd last, a couple of years down the line, setting off on a pissing-wet rainy Wednesday for a train to Redditch, to read to three men and a dog in the cornered-off children's section of the public library, then back to a B&B on the main road with a coin-operated electricity meter in the room and the world snoring champion in the bed behind the cardboard wall.

The other sad news this week is that Chelsea have won the FA Cup. You mustn't have been concentrating, because the only time you allow clubs from London to do well is in Europe. On this occasion, though, you just couldn't summon up the mental energy to stop them walking all over Middlesbrough at Wembley, and now they're making their way past Chelsea Town Hall in an open-top bus, to a civic reception.

Dennis Wise is comprehensively unlikeable, isn't he? A tennis ball on legs. If he didn't play football, he'd be the short one in East 17 or working in a fairground. It's right to think, isn't it, that Dennis Wise is what might be referred to as a 'nasty piece of work'. Also, are you the only person in Britain to think that Ruud Gullit is not the visionary genius he's cracked up to be? He's always right, but that's because he says the most obvious things, and in that respect, there's very little to separate him from Trevor Brooking. Apart from the obvious. It's possible to like Leboeuf, but he's gone and had his hair cut like Dennis Wise, so he's out. And Hughes of course, which goes without saying. Watching them all in a line at the Cup Final before kick-off was like watching the final judging at Crufts, or the Chelsea Flower Show, or an audition queue for *Chorlton and the Wheelies*.

Darren Gough has taken the first Australian wicket of the summer, but live Teletext doesn't record if he thumped the air after having the tourists' captain caught behind, or the reaction of the Western Terrace to one of their own drawing first blood. None of the several radios and crystal sets and hi-fi systems in the house receive long-wave, so every ten minutes you potter outside to listen to the commentary in the car, a performance which your next-door neighbour watches from her kitchen window. The fifth time, you're so self-conscious you take a screwdriver with you, and pretend to be fiddling about with something under the dashboard. You even think about polishing the bodywork, just so you can hang around the car without the police or an ambulance being called. Are you a moralist, or just a skinflint? Will you be the last man in the world to succumb to Sky? Like still asking for vinyl in Our Price. Like Borg and his wooden racket. Like the man in front of you in Sainsbury's last week, wanting to pay cash.

News Just In

A human heart has been found on a park bench in Rotherham.

And a court has ruled that council worker Clifford Dean did not need insurance to ride his motorized skateboard on public roads, nor did he need to wear a crash helmet. Mr Dean had been stopped by police in Bridlington, on the basis that the machine had wheels, steering, brakes, and a petrol engine, and therefore constituted a vehicle. The American-made 'go-ped', shown in the *Yorkshire Post* with Clifford flat-out at 10 m.p.h., is more of a stand-up scooter, like a metal-detector connected to a roller-skate, with a bottle of pop and a hair-drier over the back axle.

Actually, someone you knew at school had a serious accident on a similar contraption, when he fell over on to its tubular metal handlebar – minus the plastic handgrip – and uncorked his eyeball from his head. He had a glass eye fitted in its place, and for the price of fifty pence (not a small amount in those days) he'd take it out, and you could look in his head. For a pound, you could put your finger in, but he had to promise not to wink.

At the same school, the biology teacher once brought a cow's lung into the class-room. He inserted a length of Bunsen burner tube into the severed windpipe, and proceeded to inflate and deflate it by blowing into the other end, then letting the air out slowly using his thumb as a valve. It lifted and sank on the big desk under the blackboard, wheezing and sighing, back on the right side of death's door. Invited up to the front for a go, the bossiest girl in the class filled the lung to its capacity, until crimson veins stood out against its pink flesh. But in drawing breath she forgot to pinch the orange tube with her fingers, and a stream of warm, meaty air flowed back into her chest, and she ran from the room like the woman who swallowed the fly, an endless food-chain of animals erupting from somewhere inside her.

Another time, in the chemistry lab, we drew the long, black curtains, and lit every gas tap on every bench, so the little yellow flames were the only light, flickering like candles. When the teacher came in from the prep-room wearing his starched white smock and peering out through his protective glasses, we sang HAPPY BIRTHDAY, even though it wasn't his birthday, as far as we knew.

Picture This

Killing a couple of hours in Leeds, you pop into Harvey Nichols' new art supermarket, on the fourth floor of the store, just in front of the café. The paintings themselves are framed in white cardboard, wrapped in cellophane, and displayed in a rack under a photograph of the artist and a short biographical note. Ten or a dozen paintings to each artist, thirty or so artists to choose from. Flicking through them is a pretty weird experience, not unlike flicking through a selection of imported or collectable LPs at a record fair, each picture being no bigger than an album cover. The prices range from just over a hundred pounds to just less than three hundred, and as a general rule, the bigger the piece, the higher the price, which is a suspicion in itself.

You find yourself liking a couple of them, but don't think you could go as far as actually buying one. It might be to do with the feeling of flipping through posters in Athena, or birthday cards in a craft market, but in the end it's to do with context. You've never bought an original piece of contemporary art, but if you ever do, you'll expect the full works plus all the trimmings: extortion, pretension, a reactionary sensation connected with ownership, a primitive feeling of empathy with the painter, curdling with the idea that you could have done better yourself, if only you'd thought of it.

Each of the paintings in Harvey Nichols comes with a little certificate of authenticity, signed by the artist and glued to the back of the picture, and a declaration of uniqueness. One of the artists wishes to remain anonymous, since 'personal details impede an objective interpretation of the work'. Even in a gallery, a statement like that would look pretty embarrassing these days, but in a department store it looks like a tantrum.

Two artists have worked collaboratively on one painting, and represent themselves with passport-sized photographs of both their faces, spliced together. In an art supermarket, this is probably referred to as a bargain.

Property Speculation – Quarry House, Leeds

Turn right out of Harvey Nichols, walk up Briggate, turn right at the Headrow, and there it is. The first time you saw the building you'd fallen asleep on a train from York to Huddersfield. Opening your eyes just before pulling into Leeds City Station, you thought you'd woken up in Gotham City. It's massive, for one thing, and for another, it's pink. Well, pale red. Some people swear that rather than being constructed it actually landed, given that one minute it wasn't there and the next minute it most certainly was. You once thought of making a ten-minute *Building Sights* film about it for BBC2, but because that programme attempts to celebrate modern architecture rather than look sideways at it, it was a non-starter. You did get to snoop around inside the building though, which is more than most people in Leeds have managed to do, and felt as if you should file a report. It's been rumoured that Quarry House might be up for sale in the near future – maybe you fancy yourself as an estate agent, giving a guided tour of the place. Maybe you're interested in buying.

The first thing to know is that most people hate it. It's partly to do with the design – somewhere between Stalin's Palace of Culture in Warsaw and a 1950s power station – but more likely it's to do with what the building represents. It was erected at a phenomenal cost on the edge of a shitty part of town, and is home to the Department of Social Security. Local people felt as if they'd paid for it, and yet the project was a government exercise in relocation, so many of those who found work within its walls were migrants from Crawley and Croydon. Immediately, it was thought of as some kind of Trojan horse, and stories emerged of nervous employees at the end of the working day, waiting for fleets of buses to spirit them out of Leeds's twilight zone, through angry mobs, to their new homes in Wetherby, Ilkley and Harrogate. Being the DSS didn't help, and neither did the strange silver configuration on top of the building's central tower, a sort of aerial with a coil around it – art, presumably – but said to be a radar detector for tracking malingerers, scroungers and dole cheats. It was the height of the Tory reign – that didn't help either.

When you park in the city and walk down the hill towards the great red blob in the distance, you want to feel like a diplomat brokering the peace between two warring factions, but you feel like a scab, crossing the picket line. Sunlight blurs the silver pinnacle into further abstraction; it could be a lightning conductor, a crow's nest, a crucifix.

Without doubt, the outside of the building is partly responsible for the mythology that's grown up around it. It's been described as Kafka's Castle, the Alamo and the Kremlin, or as some type of fortress with its narrow windows and ramparts. It also looks a little bit like Guildford Cathedral, the way it looks in the film *The Omen*. Given its position on top of a mound at the end of Leeds's main drag there's also a touch of Capitol Hill about it – seat of power and influence, Big Brother looking down from his perch.

Some people have objected to Quarry House because it doesn't fit in with the Leedscape, but quite frankly, that has to be a compliment. The skyline of the city looks like a drawing board, where ideas of all types have been tried and tested, then built properly somewhere else. Closer to, there are statues and sculptures hanging around outside the main entrance, but it's not easy to work out the symbolism, and the sunlight bouncing around the glass façade and the polished stone slabs makes it hard to look at anything properly. Two semi-naked and classically trained council workmen tell you that the concourse will be finished off with a sculpture of a snake eating a lamb, which can be accepted as the truth, even though it sounds more like the description of a tattoo.

The approach must be designed as a public space, because of its obvious opportunities for skate-punks and graffiti artists, but the underclass haven't moved in on it just yet, and absurdly, three picnickers are putting one of the benches to its intended use. With the Leeds Playhouse sat in its lap, just to the right, there's an interesting juxtaposition of functions, though not much to separate the two architecturally.

Maybe the design and construction of Quarry House was something of a no-win situation – and not just because a department with the letters SS in its title is already on a hiding to nothing. Any restored or renovated site would probably have been wasted on the DSS because it operates behind closed doors, and would have been seen as a case of denying local people the right to their own heritage. Anything refined, ornate, delicate, or chichi would have been too ironic. As it stands, Quarry House seems to be completely in keeping with the agency it houses, the service it provides and the image it maintains – humourless, unmerciful, secretive, and rigid. Why bother to hide it?

Going into the building represents a kind of trespass or privilege, because most of the journalists who turned up when it originally opened were given the cold shoulder. You're told by the press officer that the building has two internal areas, the 'inside', where you're now standing, and the 'interior', which we'll come to later. You're ushered around a sort of perimeter corridor, and given a quick tour of the facilities: gym, pool, salon, pub, sauna – all empty – with lifeguards patrolling the unrippled water and a jukebox playing Peggy Lee's *The Folks Who Live on the Hill* to itself in the Woodpecker bar. Tetley Bitter at a pound a pint – maybe everyone's working.

The self-service area looks like a hospital shop, and the smell of chemicals from the swimming pool adds to the sensation. It's easy to imagine that the signs hanging from the ceiling say *X-ray* and *Obstetrics* rather than *Cloakroom* and *Sports Hall*. The trades-men's entrance, somewhere underneath, looks like the loading and delivery bay of a provincial shopping precinct.

The atrium is pretty impressive. Good view (you're downstairs, now) and a couple of nice places to sit and ponder with a Maxpac coffee and a mechanically dispensed Jaffa Cake. Good use of light, swanky tubular rigging in front of the window and a very tempting catwalk across the wall of glass. A definite feeling of appearing in a film on the big screen with the whole of downtown West Yorkshire as a drive-in car park.

The carpet. There was outrage in Leeds when it was announced that many thousands of pounds had been spent on a bit of a rug in one of the corridors. In fact, the purchase was made because of some government regulation insisting that a certain percentage of the cost of any public building be spent on art, and the carpet depicts a stretch of running water, symbolizing the stream over which Quarry Court was built. It's hand-woven, apparently. While you're staring at it, three high-powered executives come striding out of a meeting, roll up their trouser legs and pull off their socks, then with their shoes in their pockets, paddle over to the other side. In keeping with most rivers in West Yorkshire, the carpet contains colours not usually associated with water. The other carpets in the building are either red or blue, and indicate at a glance which sector of the building a person is lost in. It's a sort of Hansel and Gretel idea, or one taken from the floors of aeroplanes, with luminous arrows that point the way to the nearest exit during a crisis.

The courtyards are interesting, and also the water gardens, with computer-controlled mist in a morning. These are safe havens, defended space, two little glades of Arcady hidden away behind glass and stone. Quiet, windless, clean. Deserted. These areas are still finding their place. Maybe they'll feel more at home when the bonsai trees have reached their full height. At one point, you get the distinct impression of sitting in the *Blue Peter* garden.

You're well inside the interior by now, entered via a kind of rotating air-lock that might well have disinfected you, X-rayed you and imprinted your DNA with a barcode at the same time. But the journey to the heart of the building is a journey towards ordinariness. The actual office space and working environment could be anywhere. It's also surprisingly small (unless they haven't shown you everything – the 'inner interior') – a Tardis in reverse. Maybe the walls are just very thick. Even the most executive offices have nothing to offer other than a view to the east. Someone had told you that from the top of here you can see York Minster, but you can't. You can see two cooling towers comparing their waistlines, and that's your lot.

When you're pushed out through the main door, like the fat donkey out of the besieged town, the 700,000 people of Leeds lay down their weapons and drift away, back to their homes and allotments. In the evening, staff from Quarry House walk out into the city, collars loosened and sleeves rolled up above the elbows, and stroll through the parks and gardens, making plans to visit galleries, see a play or a film. They sit at pavement cafés in the last of the day's sun, penning postcards to friends and relatives back home, Down South, telling them it's safe to come and visit now, stay for the weekend maybe, have a night on the town.

Saturday Night

'Dessay. It's Sat'dy night.' Richard Whiteing, 1899

Modern Times
BBC2, 3 April 1996
Directed by Brian Hill

IAN: I'm twenty-five now. I take a lot of Ecstasy tablets, I take a lot of amphetamines, I take cocaine. Drugs is drugs, and I love 'em. Know what I mean?

[Picture: Leeds – motorway, terraces, allotments, fair, ferris wheel, ring-road, public transport, dual-carriageway, hills beyond town hall clock.]

> Leeds, where the M1 does its emergency stop,
> and the ranks of houses fall into line and number off,
> acting their age,
> and the roads go round in rings
> or spider out like varicose veins,
> and the taxis and buses are antibodies cruising the system,
> and the moors are waiting like clouds, over the next horizon.

[Arcades, Victoria Quarter, precinct, the Headrow, Harvey Nichols, Big Issue *vendor, Quarry House.]*

> Or Leeds with its new dosh,
> with its tarted-up streets and tarted-up shops,

Leeds where Harvey Nichols is coming to town,
and the Kremlin stands its ground
like a Trojan horse full of clean white collars
from Down South.

[Tracking shot: housing, empty streets.]

Or Leeds on a Saturday afternoon, beginning to cool,
Leeds in a different light, a Leeds of the mind,

[Woman hauling pram up steps of steep embankment – tortoise-shell cat sliding through fence into garden – boy watching two mongrels fighting in road.]

where a woman drags a kid
up the north face of the great pyramid,
and a Bengal tiger disappears into the foliage,
and a boy trains dogs for the Chinese State Circus.

[Traffic, rush hour – cyclist on pavement, rugby field behind.]

A motorcade speeds down the Avenue of the Americas,
and a boy rides a bike through the goalposts
and out of the known universe . . .

[JACKIE, driving.]

Each to their own, anything goes.
Jackie's a comer-in, can't get into the swing of it,
came Up North from The Smoke
but can't get a feel for it.

She's staying at home,
she's making a meal of it.

JACKIE: Well, we're going to have a salady sort of thing to start off with, and then there's a beef stew for the main course, because the people who are coming . . . well, the men, are into their food, so you've got to do something solid.

[IAN, walking.]

> Each to their own, choose your own poison,
> Ian's a big pharmaceuticals person.
> He's in
> with the chemistry set,
> and the space cadets,
> and the medicine heads . . .

IAN: I moved down here from Newcastle. I had trouble in a slashing, where I slashed a boy. Slashed him all over, across his back, in the face, stabbed him in the head . . . All for a perfectly good reason . . .

[LOLA, lifting the hem of her pleated skirt.]

LOLA: Hi!

> She's not the world's most physical guy
> but there's more to Lola than meets the eye.
> Each to their own, san fairy Ann,
> she's a wardrobe mistress, a lady's man.

LOLA: Some men find me attractive, but you never know how serious it's going to be, do you? Whether they've got a crush on a tranny, whether it's some kind of perversion or whether they're just out for a good time. I'm always getting my skirt pulled up . . .

[Mike's Carpets (converted church).]

MIKE: 'From £1.99, £2.99 and £3.99 a square yard, this is the famous Mike's Carpets, the sale starts now . . .'. Well, that was the first commercial that we did years ago, er, a bit makeshift and a bit down-market, but we weren't trying to make *Gone with the Wind* or *Ben-Hur*, we were just trying to flog a few carpets . . .

Mike Smith, the Charlton Heston of the carpet trade.
Clark Gable of the world of underlay.
In Leeds at least, he's a household name,
famous for making it hand over fist
from a bricked-up church, flogging shag-pile twist.

[P.m., headlights, streetlights, traffic lights, neon signs.]

Dreamtime in boom-town,
teatime in Yorkshire, five-o'clock shadow.
Saturday night coming in from the east like a tide
having waited all week at the edge of the world
for a green light.

[Half-eight, nine-ish, department-store windows, window shopping, shutting up shop.]

Saturday night when the back of the mind
comes into the mind's eye,
Saturday night for pleasing your own sweet self
in the city of Leeds,
for cranking it up, letting off steam.

[LOLA, watching National Lottery Live with flatmate, KYO. Screws ticket up, throws it at telly. Offers KYO a lolly.]

LOLA: Do you want a lolly, babe? Here, have a drumstick with Lola.

[JACKIE, setting the table.]

JACKIE: I've got these little place-settings ... They're French, these place-settings, they've all got a little description of the person they refer to. So for example you've got La Charmers, which is quite a nice one, and you've got Le Malicious, which is not a very nice one ... so ...

> How now brown cow: good solid grub
> with greens and carrots, gravy and spuds,
> Saturday night for pulling the cork, chewing the cud,
>
> for serving it up, passing it round,
> mulling it over, getting it down,
> Saturday night when the spirits are up,
> and the knives are out.

MALE GUEST: What's this?
JACKIE: Mad Cow Stew.
JACKIE'S HUSBAND: Looks like something out of the bottom of my golf bag. Ha ha ha ...

[MIKE in his swimming pool.]

> Back at his ranch, if a self-made man
> wants to splash out a bit on a king-size bath, well,
> he can.

MIKE: Basically I'm a Tory, but a Tory with a social conscience. I like to see people earning money, because if they're not earning money, they can't spend it with me.

[Number 96 bus (Cottingley) turning into town.]

> Nine at night in the Leeds of the mind:
> the evening well on its way,
> rounding the bend, taking the corner.

*[Two men in pub drain pint glasses – waiters in rubber-wear and
leotards – barmaids in basques and lacy underwear – two women
dancing in pub à la Status Quo.]*

> Two gods on Olympus down goblets of nectar.
> Below, in the dance-halls,
> waiters and waitresses ladle out tea and iced water,
> well-heeled ladies in lace and their thoroughbred daughters
> wait to be asked to the floor for a waltz or a polka.

[Dinner party.]

JACKIE'S HUSBAND: Noakes was there before Purves. He took
over from Trace. Trace was a pufter.

[LOLA, conducting singing outside nightclub.]

LOLA: Her name was Lola, she was a showgirl . . .

[Kisses boy on forehead.]

LOLA: There's one for your mother.

[MIKE carrying Rod Stewart outfit and guitar into pub.]

> Saturday night,
> when the shirt comes out from under the iron,
> when the perm comes out from under the dryer.
> Mike's got a sideline
> in the limelight.
> This is the night-shift after the day job.
> In with the banjo, out with the gripper-rod.

MIKE: Aye, it's fun is show business.

[*Dinner party.*]

FEMALE GUEST: Yes, but who are the presenters these days, Rick?
RICK: Bollocks, I don't know.
FEMALE GUEST: Exactly.

[*Pause.*]

RICK: But they're not pufters.

[*MIKE (voice over: 'I'm the most unracist person you'll ever, ever meet . . .') telling jokes in the pub.*]

MIKE: Pakistani waiting for a bus, and there's this dog comes and does the biggest pile of steaming shit at the side of the road . . .

[*Dinner party.*]

WIFE: How often do you smack our children?
HUSBAND: Oh . . . about once a day. Ha ha ha.
WIFE: I say what you do to your own, they do to their children.
HUSBAND: My father used to beat me with a poker and a leather belt.
WIFE: You probably deserved it.

MIKE: . . . I said who the fuck wants to go to Africa at this time of night. Ha ha ha ha . . .

[*Stretch limo right to left past camera along Briggate – Lola leaving house; wig, fun-fur coat, high-heels, feather boa – three men in baggy*

shirts and jeans, slo-mo, backlit – hot dogs being sold at side of street
– taxi – man, cig. in hand, girl in Bacofoil blouse under his arm –
nightclub queue being frisked for drugs.]

And a taxi from Armley turns into a stretch car on
  Broadway
taking the street for a ride,

And Cinders buttons her fun-fur coat and goes to the ball
in the Leeds of the mind,

and three Yorkshire astronauts
walk on the moon for the first time,
taking giant steps down Briggate for mankind,

and a garçon dishes up devils on horseback and cheese
  straws
at the Queen's garden party,

and punters take the avenue to where it's at
on wheels or shanks's pony,

and courting couples stroll the Champs-Elysées,
arm in arm, taking the air,

and everyone who's anyone arrives in style
for their own world première.

[Dinner party.]

JACKIE: If a bloke made a pass at you, you'd run a bloody mile.
JACKIE'S HUSBAND: If they make a pass at you, that's different.
That's when you smack 'em in the mouth. 'Course you do.

MIKE: . . . He says, that's the cleanest vagina I've ever seen. She
says, well, I have a woman in twice a week. Ha ha ha ha . . .

Eleven o'clock of a night
when Ian steps out in the Leeds of the mind.
He's recalling the time of his life,
remembering breaking the speed limit, passing the acid
   test,
recounting the where and the when of his personal best.

IAN: I took eighteen Ecstasy tablets. Started at six o'clock, double drop in the bath, waiting for the come up – bang, straight through. Another one in the queue, then just kept poppin' 'em. It's pleasant, that's all I can say. Just very, very pleasant. Saturday night means everything to me. If there wasn't no weekend for nightclubbing and drugs, then what's left for me?

[*Dinner party.*]

JACKIE: If someone got out a joint, I'd feel a lot better about it than watching you lot getting paralytically drunk. You should see yourselves. It's horrible.

[*LOLA, singing 'We're Off to See the Wizard', leading a trail of ravers down the street from one club to next, carrying a wand in her hand.*]

MIKE: . . . Can you recommend a good port? He said Yes, Southampton, now piss off. Ha ha ha . . .

[*Dinner party.*]

HUSBAND: When I go out for a drink, I give the responsibility of the children to you.
WIFE: How often do you think I go out for a drink?
HUSBAND: Never.

WIFE: Thank you.

[Black Maria on street corner – drunk, navel-gazing, sat on wall – couple arguing.]

2 a.m. A meat wagon waits for its cargo of meat.

A philosophy student considers
the meaning of meaning of meaning of meaning
by counting his feet.

Shadow boxing, Judy and Punch sort it out in the street.

IAN: I just took another Ecstasy tablet. You might think – the Media, right – that I'm proper off my head, but I'm in full control of my body, and I feel really nice, and I've took six tablets, not one *[holds up five fingers]* but six, and just under a quarter of amphetamine, which is whiz, and I feel super, really confident. I feel famous. You can put any woman in front of me – Pamela Anderson – and I'd rather take four E. Because drugs is drugs.

[Dinner party.]

HUSBAND: Excuse me, are you driving home tonight?
WIFE: Yes, I am.
HUSBAND: So?

[MIKE back at home. Bar. Optics. Pours himself a drink.]

MIKE: Yeah well, there we are. It's been a good night, quite pleasant, people enjoying themselves, having a nice drink. Good laugh. Cheers.

['Pop video' sequence in nightclub, superimposed with flashback scenes (in colour) – including IAN smoking joint, LOLA pruning

and preening in front of mirror, men at dinner party drinking brandy
and playing snooker on toy snooker table in dining-room after meal,
MIKE *in leopard-skin leggings singing 'Maggie May'.]*

[Door opens into ladies' toilet . . .]

> Drugs is
> your own tattoos coming alive on your skin,
> opening a door and letting a light in
> is what drugs is,
>
> what drugs is
> is talking out of your hat, waiting for the come up,
> scarecrow hair under a backwards baseball cap
> is what drugs is;
>
> drugs is
> Joshua Tetley in stiletto heels and pink pyjamas,
> a fingernail moon of a kiss-curl under a teddy-bear
>   bandanna
> is what drugs is,
>
> what drugs is
> is the bottom line of the life of Ecstasy,
> mirrors going all the way back to infinity
> is what drugs is;
>
> drugs is
> your own face looking back from a brandy glass,
> a white limo stretching from Chapeltown to Halifax
> is what drugs is,
>
> what drugs is
> is not one but six, not one but six,
> the lips and a spliff in a long French kiss
> is what drugs is;

drugs is
two puddings, trifle and mincemeat strudel,
raving beauties speeding in the little boys' room
is what drugs is,

what drugs is
is dropping six tabs and the bonus ball,
a dining-room done out as a snooker hall
is what drugs is;

drugs is
bang, straight in, four E or Pamela Anderson,
sliding a pair of lycra leopard-skin trousers on
is what drugs is,

what drugs is
is between the deep blue sea and the devil in us,
the meeting of La Charmers and Le Malicious
is what drugs is;

drugs is
your own tattoos coming alive on your skin,
opening a door and letting a light in
is what drugs is, is what drugs is . . .

[Dinner party.]

HUSBAND *[slurring words, falling off chair]* to WIFE: When I go out, I only go out minimal. Very minimal. Don't spew up on me, boy. Don't look at me like that.

[Goes over and tries to give her a kiss.]

[IAN, philosophizing, sat on pavement outside nightclub. Small hours.]

IAN: If I win the lottery, right, I'm going to have buckets and buckets and buckets of Ecstasy, right, and a big massive mansion, right, and all my friends are going to live with me, and everyone's got their own room and a bucketful of Es as well, and they just eat Es all the time, constantly E'd up, not worrying that they'll ever run out of money to buy Es. And that is the bottom line of the life of Ecstasy.

[JACKIE turning out lights, going upstairs to bed.]

JACKIE: I just think it's nice spending time with your friends.

[Empty streets, street-cleaning cart, suggestion of dawn.]

> Saturday night,
> spiralling out till Sunday morning
> arrives in the east, turns up to stop it,
> Saturday night,
> till the sun comes up
> like a swab or a pocket watch pulled from a pocket.

Photocopying

Into Huddersfield, to Xerox some poems from one of your books, to send to a friend.

You: Could you photocopy three pages out of this book, and two out of the other one?

Photocopier: You'll have to fill out a copyright form.

You: Really?

Photocopier: It's the law.

You: Actually, these are my books.

Photocopier: Doesn't matter who owns them. It's the law.

You: No, I mean they're *my* books.

Photocopier: How would you feel if you'd written them and somebody just came along and ran a load off? It's theft, that. You can either fill out those forms, or you'll have to go somewhere else.

You: Where else is there?

Photocopier: Try the library. They're not bothered.

Memorandum

Teaching for a couple of days at the school in North Yorkshire where Russell Harty used to teach. In the dining-room, over school dinner, you start chatting with one of the masters, who tells you that Yorkshire air is no good for his Jaguar, and is causing some of the chrome to rust. He goes on, 'I had it in South London before, but you can't drive a Jag around South London. Get to the end of the street and there's a thousand coons jumping all over it.'

You don't know why he's made this statement, and you're not quick enough in mind or body to know what to say, how to react. An image of Grace Jones comes to mind, but you can't convert it into a sentence or a course of action. So you're just making a note of it, here, in writing, until you think what to do for the best.

Tour of Duty

Williamsburgh, Virginia. Reading at College of William and Mary, one of several 'oldest' colleges in America. Site of earliest settlers from England. Population of town – 10,000, including 5,000 university staff and student body, plus 5,000 heritage guides in cheesecloth blouses, calico britches and rope shoes, selling honey and tobacco. Actual population of town – about twenty black men, standing around on street corner waiting for world to change. Jamestown, half a dozen miles away on banks of river is even older and even more historic and boasts heritage theme park. Consists mainly of descendants of five or six North American Indians whose forebears escaped genocide at hands of settlers, rubbing sticks together to make fire. Also Vietnam veterans in period costume demonstrating loading and firing of musket ball in unerringly enthusiastic manner. All heritage guides speak perceived version of seventeenth-century rural English – like being served in Burger King in Lincoln in 1650.

Amherst, Massachusetts. Pronounced Am-erst, but told off so many times for dropping aitch, can't say it properly. Sitting in bar on night of total eclipse of moon. Ask bartender if drinks can be taken outside, to watch it.

> *Bartender:* Sure, but you really don't have to.
> *You:* Why's that?
> *Bartender:* It's live on Channel 61.

(Bartender flicks TV over with remote. Picture of full moon beginning to be eaten by shadow.)

You: All the same . . .

Bartender: The way I see it, it's kinda total, so there's nothing to see. Right?

You (going outside): Right.

Princeton, New Jersey. Massive stone-built campus in period style. Like Camelot. Staying at Nassau Inn. Restaurant and bar lined with photographs of college football teams, famous graduates and ex-professors, including Albert Einstein. Video trivia machine next to toilets:

Q: Pick a Category – Sport, History, Science, Literature, Sex.
A: Sex.
Q: Swallowing cum causes plaque. True or false?

Einstein sucks on his pipe, scratches his head.

Later, watching telly in bed in Nassau Inn. Sound of headboard banging against wall in adjoining room; turn telly up. More banging; turn telly up more. Ongoing banging; turn telly up even more. Telephone rings. Receptionist: Could I turn TV down please – man in next room can't get to sleep. He's been banging on wall but TV gets louder and louder. Thank you.

Baltimore, Maryland. Internet, the *Huddersfield Examiner*. An eighty-year-old man has died after choking on his full English breakfast. The octogenarian was found slumped motionless in his chair after his meal, which included a starter portion of porridge. Coroner Roger Whittaker has recorded a verdict of death by natural causes.

New York, New York. Internet, the *Yorkshire Post*. Robert Ancliff of Bradford was left with 'a sour taste in his mouth' when he read the note left by his milkman on his doorstep. The previous day, Mr Ancliff had typed a polite letter of complaint, asking what had happened to the extra pint of milk he had requested. The handwritten reply read: 'I did get your milk delivered. It must have been stolen, so kiss my f****** a***.' The milkman has quit without notice and has not been seen since. A company spokesman has apologized, and Mr Ancliff has been given complimentary milk for his trouble.

Degrees of Separation

To Portsmouth. Mum, Dad and your sister, Hilary, want to come, so we drive down in one car, a journey that takes in Newbury with its many traffic lights and roundabouts. Of course, you're against the Newbury Bypass on principle – the principle being that you don't have to drive through the town more than once every five years.

You've got lots of memories from your days as a geography student in Portsmouth, many of them bad memories, such as the time you were beaten up in a pub for looking like a 'skate', skate being Pompey slang for sailor. Six of us sheltered in an alcove in a pub as locals threw pint pots, one of them taking a slice out of your scalp just above the hairline, still visible if the barber gets carried away with the clippers.

A second bad memory involves violence of a reverse kind, though its direction was the same in the sense that you were on the receiving end again. Three of us were sitting one afternoon on the balcony of a flat in Western Parade, overlooking the Common and the shore. The building was having a face-lift at the time and was covered in scaffolding. Four sailors swaggering along the street in their flares heard us laughing somewhere up above them, and must have thought we were laughing at them. As if. Five seconds later they were halfway up the rigging with us scrambling back inside the room and trying to lock the catch on the window. When they reached the balcony they booted the glass out of the frame, slapped us around a bit, then shinned down the scaffolding with the bottle of whisky from on top of the bookcase and the beer from the fridge. You wonder sometimes if this kind of internecine warfare still goes on in Portsmouth, between the thugs on the estates and the bell-bottomed matelots on shore leave, with the students in the middle, puny and innocent, caught in the cross-fire.

On the morning of the ceremony, you go along to your parents' hotel room, and Mum tells you she's going to iron your shirt. This isn't because she thinks you're inept, although that does come into it at some level; it's because she doesn't want you standing on stage in 100 per cent cotton with 90 per cent creases, showing her up. You rip off your tie, drag the shirt over your head and watch Teletext for five minutes as she rigs up an ironing board using the dressing table and a bath towel. Steam rises to the ceiling. Dad smokes his pipe through the open window, avoiding the smoke alarm.

Outside it's summer, and it's hot. In the taxi on the way to the Guildhall, you scribble the last few lines of a poem on the back of the invitation, then make your way to the robing-room, where someone kits you out in a purple cloak, an off-the-shoulder sash and a large velvet beret. You look like a cross between the Archbishop of Canterbury, the Queen of the May, and Toulouse-Lautrec.

Mum, Dad and Hilary are issued with numbered tickets, and disappear up the back steps. The organ starts playing, and you file into the Main Hall behind the University politburo – a party of a few dozen, led by the man who carries the official mace, a large silver baton in the shape of a pepper grinder.

It's summer. It's hot. The gown is very heavy and the hat acts like the stopper on a thermos flask. Your coronation involves standing for about half an hour as one of the officials chews through three or four of your poems, none of them very short, and none of them, it occurs to you at that moment, any good.

You feel as if you're melting, like one of those candles in the shape of a choirboy, with a burning wick making its way through his body and a little pool of wax at his feet. You think of all the students in the hall with their brilliant degrees in astro-physics or architecture or even English, thinking, 'Who the fuck's this clown?' You shuffle over to the lectern and read the poem.

> Going back down south to the mouth of the port
> for the first time in an age,
> I thought that things would have turned or turned about,
> but nothing had changed.
>
> The hovercraft still ironed a pleat to the Isle of Wight
> and skirted the beach.
> Still rusting away at the end of the street,
> the battleship grey
> of Her Majesty's fleet.
> The rent still hadn't been paid in Nightingale Road
> and Western Parade.
>
> From the stage at this year's Graduation,
> looking back through time,
> I clocked some blank-faced kid in the congregation,
> rubbing his eyes:
>
> it was me, as seen through two or three degrees of
>   separation,
> stunned with surprise,
> looking up at himself through a twelve-year divide
> of letters and lines.

You shake hands with Lord Palumbo, and it's all over. We troop out the way we trooped in, and you see your family up in the gods, nodding their heads, shaking hands with the people next to them. Someone in the centre aisle, a man you don't know, somebody's parent probably, leans over and says, 'Well done, lad,' in an accent that might be Sheffield or Leeds.

Backstage, you hand back the togs like Mr Benn in the cartoon after his little adventure. We move on to the Administration Block for something to eat and something to drink, and all your old lecturers are very generous for saying how much they remember you without saying why. Across the other side of the room is Sir Terence Conran, receiving *his* Honorary Doctorate in the afternoon sitting of the proceedings. Sir Terence has a woman with him, a PA presumably, who acts as a sort of semi-conductor between him and the rest of the world. At the crucial moment she steps into the gap between us and 'reminds' him who you are. You're grateful for the intervention. It saves going through the charade of him complimenting you on your poems, which he can't have read, and you congratulating him on his latest settee.

Getting changed back at the hotel, you pull off the white cotton shirt without unbuttoning it, and come face to face with the label inside the collar. It isn't yours. It's your dad's.

All Quiet on the Western Terrace

Second Day of the Fourth Test at Headingley – edited highlights:

i) The five monks, twelve Vikings, three Quakers, two clowns and four assorted farmyard animals pushing through the turnstiles, two by two, into the Western Terrace.

ii) The blue blazers, day-glo bibs and huge, pub-fighting faces of the security forces, cattle-ranching the Western Terrace.

iii) The spontaneous chant of 'You've got a lampshade, on your head' to the tune of 'He's got the whole world, in his hands' as a man in a pink and emerald halter-neck frock walks on to the Western Terrace with a handbag in one hand and a pint in the other, wearing a lampshade on his head.

iv) The Western Terrace not startled into panic as the last seven English wickets fall in just over an hour for thirty-four measly runs to a man with a goatee beard and two gold curtain hooks for earrings.

v) At least twenty men in one of the arches under the Western Terrace, watching horse-racing on a portable telly.

vi) A streaker, springing from deep third man on the far side of the ground, hurdling the wicket at the non-striker's end, finally up-ended by six stewards on the long-leg boundary, thirty yards short of the safe haven of the Western Terrace.

vii) The Western Terrace not startled into panic as Graham Thorpe puts down Matthew Elliott at slip, a dolly, and scrambles after the ball like a man chasing precious ashes spilt from a box in a hurricane.

viii) Some bright spark on the Western Terrace shouting, 'I'm Spartacus,' followed by thirty or forty shouts of 'I'm Spartacus' as security guards try to identify the man responsible for throwing a plastic beer bottle on to the field at deep square leg.

ix) The spontaneous chant of, 'Three pounds an hour, you're earning three pounds an hour' to the tune of 'Guantanamera', as security guards move in to eject a man from the Western Terrace for shouting 'Fuck off you Aussie cunt' as Matthew Elliott raised his bat to the sky in celebration of his second Test century.

x) Daisy the pantomime cow, grazing the outfield, ram-raided into the advertising hoardings by security guards, causing a sort of cracking, sort of bone-breaking crunching noise, audible even from the Western Terrace.

xi) The Western Terrace after close of play, in the last of the sunshine, as a plastic glass wobbles drunkenly in the breeze, teeters on the lip of a wooden bench, then pukes its inch and a half of flat, warm beer on to the concrete steps, where the spineless liquid drains away downhill in the direction of the end of summer.

Quiz Night Down at the Club

Question-master: Which is the most active volcano in Europe?
Contestant: When you say Europe, how far are you going?
Question-master: How far do you want to go?
Contestant: Iceland?
Question-master: Oh no, not that far.

Mum's Gone to Iceland

Water is the theme for the day. It's raining when the alarm goes off and you look out of the bedroom window, but by the time we're on the M62 the roads are drying out, and it's just coming dawn. You follow the signs through Bradford and Yeadon, overtaking the milk-floats and the first buses of the morning. When we arrive at the airport, a security guard is holding up a cardboard sign saying ICELAND, with an arrow directing us into a separate car park. Mum joins the check-in queue in the terminal, and you sidle off to the Thomas Cook's office to change fifty pounds sterling into not very many Icelandic Krona. Like all unfamiliar currency, the crisp, dry notes look like toy money, and you slip what little there is of it into your wallet. The only banknotes that actually feel like real money, you reckon, are dollars, which are nearly always dog-eared and smell of sweat – presumably the authentic odour of the American back-pocket. Mum hasn't got to the front of the line yet, so you sit to one side, watching everyone gossiping and laughing, apparently unaware that it's still only six o'clock in the morning.

When your mother asked you if you wanted to go with her on the *Yorkshire Post* readers' day trip to Iceland, your first thoughts were that you did not. You'd been to Iceland a couple of years ago and had a very trance-like and introspective three or four weeks, feeling you were in another life, or having one of those experiences that happens outside or parallel to everyday passages of time. To go again on a Wednesday from Leeds/Bradford airport and be back in time for a drink might somehow break the spell, or make what you'd felt before redundant, idiotic even. But when you'd checked the date of the trip and seen that it coincided with National Poetry Day, it felt like the perfect alternative to doing something embarrassing and unprofitable in the name of literature. So you'd stumped up the hundred and odd quid there and then, and put your name on the list.

You'd also thought that there might only be a handful of us, making the journey in a half-empty twin-prop commandeered for the day from an aviation museum somewhere in the region. But the concourse is packed with people, most of them retired it looks like, all of them wearing a little Monarch Airlines tag on the end of a piece of string, like a rip-cord. As well as this mark of identification, we've also been told in the itinerary to wear 'suitable clothing', and people's interpretation of this says a great deal about the Iceland they think they're visiting. 'Suitable' ranges from Gortex cagoules, North Face rucksacks and strap-on compasses, to M&S car-coats and driving gloves, to pac-a-macs and five-penny transparent rain-hoods available from all good newsagents and tobacconists. For Mr Green, a seventy- or eighty-year-old complete with name-badge presumably sewn on by an anxious relative, 'suitable' means a thick woollen suit, a thin woollen tie, a hand-knitted waistcoat and a pair of stout leather brogues. He stands next to you, rummaging in his pockets. Somebody calls his name over the tannoy, but he can't hear it because of the mounds of black, wiry hair growing out of each ear, and the Sony Walkman playing tinnitus at full volume. You picture him at the end of the day, an Icelandic flag pinned to his tie, queuing up in the duty-free with a bag of toffees and a half-bottle of Navy rum in his basket.

The theme for the day is water. The woman behind the counter in the airport café warms the teapot with hot steam before filling it and mashing the tea. She says 'Ta' instead of 'Thank you'. The five or six men in suits flying off on business trips look uncomfortable in and amongst the rabble of hikers and day-trippers, and they congregate around one table, willing their mobile phones to ring. Through the window, a heron punts across the runway and touches down on the golf-course on the other side. Sandwich boxes have already been broken into, and the whiff of potted meat kept in plastic containers begins to fill the air. Eventually we get the call, file across the Tarmac, and climb a pair of glorified step-ladders on to the plane. A woman in a knee-length quilted anorak has trouble stowing an aluminium deck-chair in the overhead locker. Mr Green is sitting in somebody else's seat. We look around for anyone we know, but surprisingly, there isn't anybody. The plane is full. The ratio of pensioners to poets is roughly three hundred and fifty to one. The temperature in Reykjavik is two degrees centigrade, and our estimated time of arrival is 9 a.m. There's an atmosphere on board like the beginning of a works outing, the sort of trip that might end in community singing and a whip-round for the driver.

There are seven tour buses ready and waiting outside Keflavik airport, one for Reykjavik only, three for the guided tour, and three for the guided tour including the Viking Lunch. Mum thought that twenty quid for a reindeer steak and baked Alaska was 'a bit on the pricey side', so we've brought sandwiches and a thermos, and we climb on to one of the coaches, pleased that about a hundred and fifty reasonable-looking people evidently thought the same thing. The first stop, on the outskirts of the capital, is a thermally heated open-air swimming baths, and we're encouraged to stand in front of a glass wall taking photographs of Icelandic citizens chugging up and down a twenty-five-metre pool. In the 'hot-pots' along the side, men and women seem to be boiling themselves in circular tubs of bubbling water, ranging from 36 to 44 degrees C, colour-coded from flesh-pink to lobster-red. You're the first back on the bus, apart from Mr Green who never got off, who snores with his head back and mouth wide open, music still leaking from his ear-plugs.

The convoy of blue coaches – fifties-looking, charabanc things – circles the city before making for the great white spire on the horizon. 'If you see a strange-looking building in Iceland, it's probably a church,' says the tour-guide. It makes a change from West Yorkshire, where if you see a church it's probably a discount carpet centre or an architect's house. We tumble off, snoop around, make a donation and climb back on board. Then it's lunchtime, and you drag Mum along to a café on the main street, where you gave a reading when you were here last time. We order coffee, and sneak sandwiches out of a bag, breaking them in half under the table.

We see a lot of each other, but you can't remember the last time you spent a whole day with your mother – just you and her. It's a thought that dawns on both of us, privately, as we sit in the window of the Café Islandus Solon in Reykjavik, Iceland, smuggling handfuls of ham roll into our mouths. The last time you had this much of her to yourself was before you started school, before she started work, and now she's retired we're picking up where we left off, with just a small matter of thirty years in between. Strangely enough, her last job was at the village infants' school, the same place she deposited the screaming cry-baby that was you at the age of three or four. You hated it: the big hall like a church with the seats taken out, the smell of sawdust, the half-pint bottles of milk warming up on the fire-escape all morning, the cloakrooms, the weird children who didn't mind being dumped in a life-size doll's house with other weird children all day – what was the matter with them? Footballs were banned from the playground, so we played with stones – you've told people this fact and they've looked sideways at you, as if you've misremembered it, which you haven't, or as if the school was some terrible, palaeolithic hell-hole, which it wasn't.

When Mum retired, they threw a bit of a party in the school, and one of the teachers took a big bunch of keys from a hook and showed me around. Music from the piano followed us up the stone staircase, like the stairwell in a tower, then past the head teacher's office with its glass front, like an old sweet shop, then into the triangular attic room with the fire-escape and windows in the ceiling. You thought you'd feel all the obvious things, about how small everything looked now and how safe and tidy. Bang your head on the beams maybe. But you could smell the sawdust, still taste the thick, warm milk at the back of your throat. You remembered the thunderstorm one afternoon when the sky was bottle green and the lights went out and we all sheltered under a desk as the lightning hunted the sky for the metal flagpole on the roof above us.

In the darkness, you looked down into the playground and told the story about the stone football, but the teacher said, 'That doesn't sound right to me.' A cracker went off in the hall underneath us, or a bottle of champagne. We all ended up in one of the classrooms, sat on the tiny seats with our knees up in front of our faces, you and your dad pouring beer from the miniature plastic teapot into miniature cups. Some of the weird children were there, thirty years older, still looking as if everything was perfectly normal.

The tour bus makes another circuit of the city. You point at buildings and streets from the window, saying this is where such and such happened last time, this is where you met so and so. Mum puts her hand over her mouth as she yawns. Asleep, Mr Green goes past on the wrong bus in the opposite direction. It starts to rain and the guide says, 'We have a saying in Iceland: if you don't like the weather – wait a minute.' Half an hour later, we're travelling under a clear blue sky along a single-track road across acres of broken stones. The woman behind you has become obsessed with the opening and closing of the back door of the coach. Stopping at the sulphur pools, she leans over to Mum, saying, 'The back door's open.' Mum nods in agreement. 'They haven't opened it this time,' she announces at the fish-processing plant, then, 'Open again,' at the president's house. The president, as it happens, is not at home, which is just as well for him because half the party go lumbering across the lawns and gawp through the windows. No doubt he saw the fleet of blue buses trundling up towards him out of town, and slipped out the back, scooting along the spit of land in his Nissan Micra, making for the interior.

The last stop of the day, and also the highlight of the trip for which we've forked out an extra fiver, is the Blue Lagoon. As the bus climbs over the last volcanic hill, we see the lagoon about a mile in front of us, a cloud of steam rising from the green, opalescent water. On its own it would be a miracle, an oasis of colour in a landscape of inert, grey stones. But the massive power-plant behind it somehow deadens the effect, especially when we hear that the efficacious water we're about to immerse ourselves in is a by-product from a heat-transfer process. The guide explains that the naturally hot water from under the earth is 'too much in clogging and clagging' to be put through pipes, so it's used to heat surface water, then drained into a pond. When changing huts are erected around the pond, it becomes a pool, and when the rich minerals of the earth's interior are added into the equation, it becomes a spa.

You strip off in one of the cubicles and follow the slotted wooden walkway outside. There are a couple of seconds in which you're conscious of standing in the open air in a freezing wind in a pair of trunks in front of a power station in Iceland, and then the warmth from the pool drifts up the gang-plank towards you, and you take the plunge.

It's very, very hot. You swim out to the middle, and tread water with half a dozen people from the bus. Mum's face looks the way it does when she cooks Christmas dinner – red cheeks, hair wet with steam. Mr Green sits on one of the salt-coloured islands like a cormorant on a rock. Those who didn't bring a swimming costume watch from the pier, stamping their feet to keep warm. Those of us in the water breathe the magic vapour to the bottom of our lungs, feel the precious crystals between our toes, let the electric-blue elixir draw the aches and pains from swellings and creaky joints, and loll about like seals after feeding time, contemplating eternal life.

It's just gone eleven when we land back in Yorkshire. There's a hold-up on the runway, then we have to queue outside the building in a light drizzle before passing through passport control, then have to queue again at the customs desk. Mum gets irritated with the wait, and says something, and the woman in front in a green headscarf turns round and says, 'Better safe than sorry.'

'I suppose so.'

A couple of minutes later, a man with a pale white face, carrying his glasses in his hands, walks towards the woman in the headscarf and puts his arm around her shoulder.

'Gary, what are you doing here?'

'Mary, you'd better come with me. Come on, love.'

She lets out a little giggle of surprise, but when she sees that he isn't laughing, she looks up at him for some kind of explanation.

'What is it?'

'Come on, Mary, love.'

He guides her to a door at the side of the concourse, and pushes it open. Inside the small room, two younger women move forward to comfort her, and behind them a policeman, and behind the policeman, a priest. The door closes. The queue moves slowly forward, and as we pass the room, we hear the sound of crying.

Over the Top into Lancashire

Helping somebody move house, driving a lorry through Lees, you pull up as a kid steps out on to the pedestrian crossing. You can't remember his name but you know his face. You were the duty officer at Oldham Magistrates when he was sentenced. As a juvenile, he stood silently in front of the witness box with his mother at his side, waiting for the decision. The chief magistrate that day was a dark-haired woman in her fifties. A few months before, you'd been sitting behind her at a liaison meeting as someone from Probation tried to explain the benefits of Community Service. She leaned across to one of her colleagues and whispered in a loud voice, 'Me, I just send them all to prison.'

The boy waited, staring at the ceiling, as the magistrates filed back into court from the retiring-room and took their places on the bench. She'd only just got the words 'custodial sentence' out of her mouth when he leaned forward, extended his arm towards her, offered the thin, white patch of his wrist, then dragged a razor blade across it with his other hand.

Sprung from its normal circuit, blood is a wild and lively substance, and carries within it one last effort of will, like the leap of a man from a burning house. There was a moment of suspension, like in a painting, a Chagall, with bodies hanging in mid-air: the fat policeman dropping down from above; the magistrate diving sideways for the door with a thick, oily scream flowing from her mouth; the boy with his hand still raised, his long crimson arm reaching out towards her with its fingertips on fire.

All Points North

You watch him stride from one side of the road to the other with his hands in his pockets, as the green man on the pedestrian crossing flashes on and off then turns to red. The lights change, and you move off.

Points of Reference – North

Devised by Simon Armitage and Sue Roberts
Radio 4, 4 December 1996 and 15 September 1997

Patrick Moore: People often ask me how you find the North Star. Well, it's quite easy. First of all, it's always in the north. I think most people can probably recognize the constellation of the Great Bear, or the Plough, whatever you call it, and the two end stars of the Plough show the way to the Pole Star. And the Plough is so near the Pole it never sets. Whenever the sky is clear and dark, you can always see the Plough somewhere, and you can find the Pole Star from there.

Group Captain David W. Broughton, Director of the Royal Institute of Navigation: In the northern hemisphere one can anchor the sky on Polaris – the entire sky rotates around that star, and that is, I think, something that locates one a little bit . . . makes one feel comfortable.

Patrick Moore: The Earth spins round on its axis of rotation, and northward the axis points to a position known as the North Celestial Pole, and Polaris is within one degree of that. So the sky appears to go round Polaris once in twenty-four hours. There's nothing special about Polaris itself; it's a fairly remote, fairly luminous star, but it owes its importance to us because it is in that position in the sky.

David Broughton: A very long time ago direction was taken from the whereabouts of the sun and the stars etc . . .

Dr Gloria Clifton, Head of Navigational Instruments, National Maritime Museum: . . . then probably sometime between the first and sixth century A D the Chinese discovered that if you magnetized a needle with a piece of lodestone, which is a naturally magnetic iron ore, it naturally orientated itself north and south . . .

David Broughton: . . . which started the business of producing a form of magnetic direction indicator, or a compass . . .

Gloria Clifton: . . . and the Italians in the Middle Ages used compasses which were marked with the initials of the eight principal winds; there was the Tramontane, or the North, which blew north across the mountains . . .

The children of St Andrews Primary School, Leeds:
The north wind doth blow,
and we shall have snow,
and what will poor Robin do then, poor thing?

Ian McGaskill: Although we have this illusion that the northerly wind is the wind that brings snow, it's not really true at all. We get so much shelter from these mountain masses through the British Isles, that it's only the fringes that get much in the way of snow from the northerly wind. Inland it's crisp and it's clean – the weather's come straight from the North Pole . . . you can see for miles and miles and miles, or even kilometres and kilometres and kilometres . . .

Ted Hughes: They have a proverb in Devon: Knaves and foul weather come out of the north.

George Chetwynd: The map of course tells us that England is a very small country, measuring only about 420 miles from north to south. The northern counties amount to roughly a third of it; they comprise Northumberland, Cumberland, Durham, Westmorland, Yorkshire, Lancashire, and Cheshire.

Vox pop: I was brought up in West Yorkshire, I went to University in Sheffield, so I tended to think I was very much in the North, you know, and that there was this clear divide, and I think I thought anything down from the Humber was South . . .

> *Song of the South: South song:*
> *below the belt of the Mason–Dixon Line.*
> *Old Man River song,*
> *M i double s, i double s, i double p i;*
> *Carter, ruling the world in a southern drawl;*
> *Jack Daniels and Jim Beam,*
> *slugging it out in a bar-room brawl;*
> *Sue Ellen, knocking it back for breakfast down on the farm;*
> *a man in a white cotton sheet burning a cross on the lawn;*
> *strange tree hanging a strange fruit out on its arm;*
> *all that jazz – tobacco and cane,*
> *cotton and maize;*
>
> *Song of the South; South song:*
> *song of the kangaroo with its built-in purse*
> *and boxing gloves and size-ten shoes;*
> *song of the eucalyptus brewing its flammable oil and fumes;*
>
> *song of the great white shark and the Barrier Reef;*
> *song of the Opera House and Bondi Beach;*
> *song of the dingo at night on the camp-site,*
> *baring its teeth;*
> *song of the rotary drier;*

song of the spider under the toilet seat;

song of the dreamtime,
dream songs crossing the desert shield like power-lines;
song of Bradman's average rounded down to 99.9;
song of the great red rock at one with the sun
at dawn and dusk;
song of seven trailers full of fluffy white merinos,
pulled by one truck;
song of Queen and Commonwealth; Qantas; Cook;

song of a land with a continent propped in its porch;
song of a continent snug in its country's pouch;

song of the South; South song:
Bogart and Hepburn crewing a boat from the land to the sea,
under their own steam;
dirge of the cargo of Livingstone's body
carried in salt back to Westminster Abbey;

blues of the second-hand gun and the refugee;
ballad of Live Aid;
hymn of the slave-trade;

anthem of Kilimanjaro, flat on its back
with its mouth in the sky sucking milk from the mist;
chant of a million Zulus shaking their fists
at Michael Caine;
nursery rhyme of the cradle of life, Lucy and Nutcracker man
getting up from their pits;

hue and cry of the Outspan orange, giving the pip;
moan of the horn of the African rhino,
ground into dust for a Chinese erection;
psalm of the labour of Nelson Mandela,
sweeping the floor in a general election;

song of the Kruger, song of the rand;
Kurtz going mad in the dark of his heart;

Zebra, Sahara, Limpopo, Zambezi, Soweto
and Nellie the Elephant song;
song of the Nile snaking back to the source of itself,
but which one?

George Chetwynd: If you're looking at it from where we are, in the north–north-east, from the Scottish border down to Scarborough ... this is my sort of parish ... then the North really ends somewhere round about, er, Northallerton, Thirsk, somewhere ... Richmond? I really writhe, I won't say with anger, but certainly with dismay, when people talk about the North being Manchester, and Leeds. This isn't the North at all.

Song: The Fall 'Hit the North'

Stewart McConie: Good evening. This is Stewart McConie up here in the North of England. I don't want to descend into the realm of sentimental cliché, but how nice to leave behind the dirty metropolis full of men in red braces and Christopher Biggins-style glasses drinking designer water and selling pork-belly futures down mobile phones, and to get off the train instead to be met by men in mufflers and flat caps, and rosy-faced street urchins, sparking clogs and rolling Eccles cakes down the cobbled streets. And those wonderful northern rituals: Pie Thursday, the Burnage Tattoo ('Mam' and 'Dad' across the forehead), and every week – a great tourist attraction – the changing of the Man City manager ...

Vox pop: I think the North starts when you look out of a train window and you see a lot of terraced streets. *Coronation Street*'s left a great mark on me as a Londoner. That's what I think the North looks like . . .

John Braine: I speak with authority on this subject, even with a degree of rueful pride, for I am partly responsible for the present image of the North. If I hadn't written *Room at the Top*, the film of that title would not have been made, and the myth would not have been given shape. For the purpose of the film, only the harsher aspects of the northern landscape were essential; those high chimneys, those smoke-blackened stone buildings, those precipitous cobbled streets had a life of their own. The clear river effervescent with fish, the woods and pastures encircling the town and the moors and hills beyond – all this, and much more, had to be left out.

> *North, nought degrees nought,*
> *upstairs above and overhead,*
> *the hat, the hair, from here*
> *Three Peaks, Lyke Wake, Pennine Way.*
>
> *North, nought degrees nought,*
> *coal, soot, worsted, gas,*
> *plate glass,*
> *shire – derived from share,*
> *Ribble, Eden, Calder, Wear, and Aire.*
>
> *Salt, grouse, millstone grit,*
> *lead and slate,*
> *cotton, woollen, iron, lace,*
> *meat and gravy,*
> *Hindley, Brady.*
>
> *North, nought degrees nought,*
> *Rievaulx, Fountains, Stoodley Pike,*
> *alder, pine,*

nails and hinges, bobbins, spools,
electro-plated knives and tools . . .

North, nought degrees nought,
the scalp, the cranium, the cap, the skull,
Sheffield, Bradford, Blackburn, Preston, Grimsby, Hull . . .

Alan Bennett: I think the language is quite important. People in the North seem to me to enjoy their language . . . they enjoy the way they speak, and for all their lives are . . . certainly nowadays I think much harder than down here, maybe they enjoy that, though that might sound a patronizing thing to say. People tend to imagine that a northern English is simply standard English with a sort of dirty dishcloth sort of accent . . . and it isn't. The actual structure of the sentences is different, the emphasis comes at the end of the sentence. I mean, they'll say 'He's not a bad looking feller is that.' They kind of invert things.

Francis Spufford: In the eighteenth century, north as a slang word means 'canny'; it's an insult, it comes from 'canny Yorkshireman', I think, because the people who are using that word are thinking within the British Isles – that's their scope. 'Too far north' means too canny by half, you're going to steal my horse, go away.

Rowan Williams, Bishop of Monmouth: Until fairly recently, about two or three decades ago, in the liturgy of the Roman Catholic Church and some Anglican Churches, when the deacon in the holy communion service went to read the gospel, he would do it on the north side of the church. And indeed, sometimes facing the north wall, because the North was regarded as the area that hadn't yet heard the gospel. The dark region. And that explains also why certain classes of people were buried on the north side of churchyards – the not-very-respectable ones, the unbaptized, the suicides . . .

Francis Spufford: By the mid nineteenth century, north has changed its meaning, and it's become a sailor's word, as the world expands as news comes back from over the sea, and it now means 'neat', as in spirits. A drink is 'due north' if it's completely neat. You can say 'Another degree north, steward,' meaning don't stint, put some more whisky in that. And you can also say 'too far north', which means completely, hopelessly, incapably drunk, lost somewhere up there in the Arctic of booze.

Rowan Williams: . . . so in that context the North stands for something rather sinister, and it's a curious inversion of what you find in bits of the Old Testament. In one of the psalms, Mount Zion, the hill on the top of the mountain where Jerusalem stands, is metaphorically called the Far North – it's the place where God is.

Stanley Ellis: . . . the wind, arriving at land after three thousand miles of ocean, seems to blow endlessly.

> *Question: where are linen goods and sailcloth made?*
> *Question: how are the mountains of Scotland arranged?*
> *Draw a sketch map of the peaks and plains.*
>
> *Question: can you make a list of the bays and capes?*
> *Question: which of the glens is the most fertile?*
> *Which of the lochs is the longest and most beautiful?*
>
> *Which cairn, which isle, which rock, which mineral?*
>
> *Sound of Mull, Dunnet Head,*
> *John o'Groats, Firth of Forth,*
> *Mull of Oa, Scapa Flow,*
> *Moray Firth, Little Minch,*
> *Sound of Monach, Seven Hunters,*
> *Sound of Harris, Butt of Lewis,*

East Fife five, Forfar four.

So on. So forth.

Shipping Forecast: Dogger, Fisher, easterly, five or six. Increasing gale eight in Dogger . . .

Simon Wilson, Tate Gallery: How can you tell that this is northern light? Well, first of all the colour of the sea. It's a cold blue, the sun shining through grey clouds, blue-grey clouds. So it's this very very cold light. And right out on the horizon, the blue of the sea which is already very dark nearer to you, becomes almost blue-black, it becomes almost quite inky. I've just crossed the Atlantic Ocean on the *QE2*, and right out in the North Atlantic the sea is blue-black, and it's very sinister. Now, if you were to be looking west . . .

> *West as it was, West as it went:*
> *Sir Walter Raleigh in Richmond, Virginia, smoking a joint;*
> *Drake bumming a ride to the Golden Gate*
> *in Crimplene flares and an Afghan coat;*
> *Lewis and Clark playing grunge in a West Coast bar –*
> *Clark on drums, Lewis on lead guitar;*
>
> *West as it was, West as it went:*
> *Maradona wielding a pickaxe,*
> *digging bird-shapes into the Nazca Plain;*
> *Cortez in the World Cup, side-fisting the ball into the net;*
> *Pizarro laundering drug money*
> *into an offshore bank account;*
>
> *Che Guevara steering the Santiago*
> *through the Cape of Eleven Thousand Virgins,*
> *through the Magellan Strait;*

All Points North

West as it was, West as it went:
Nixon smoking Geronimo's pipe;
Sitting Bull, knifed in a heroin deal
on the Lower East Side;
the last Mohican looking for fun, companionship and love
in the small-ad section of the New York Times –
time-wasters need not apply;

Neil Armstrong buried at Wounded Knee;
O.J. having a sleepless night
in a dream by Martin Luther King;
Montezuma reading Weldon Kees;
Video night at the Alamo – Mae West in I'm No Angel,
Diamond Lil, *and* Sex.

West as it was, West as it went:
Leifur Eiriksson toasting himself with a new world white;
La Long Carabine with Kennedy's face in his rifle sights,
larger than life;
Columbus executed by the Sandinistas;
Emily Dickinson riding a Harley, feeding a parking meter.

Shipping Forecast: . . . Increasing severe gale nine at times. Fair Isle, Faroes, south-east Iceland, south-east six, occasionally gale eight in Faroes and south-east Iceland at first . . .

Caroline Wolf: And the farthest point is Point Hope. And that's as far north-west as you can go on the North American continent. And it's quite a feeling to stand on the Point and watch the ocean crash constantly . . .

Song: 'Way Up North'

Caroline Wolf: It's called the Last Frontier, and in so many ways it is. Within a half-hour walk, I can't see town any more, and in all directions all I can see is the curvature of the earth. To see the Northern Lights and to see the changing of the seasons . . . it's so . . .

Ian McCaskill: The Northern Lights are very attractive if you can see them . . . I think you've got to be quite far North.

Caroline Wolf: The Northern Lights have bands . . . like around Fairbanks they see them in reds and purples and . . . we usually see them just in pinks and greens and whites. But about a month ago I was walking across tundra . . . and from the horizon comes this big, sort of whitish arm, with fingers just squishing the stars between them, and it was the Northern Lights, but I had that feeling that it was a hand reaching out and playing with the sky above.

Ian McCaskill: I understand it's just an interaction of radioactive outbursts from the sun with the higher levels of our atmosphere. For some reason, because of the magnetic configuration around our globe, those brightly coloured illuminations tend to happen around the poles.

David Broughton: Once you start approaching the high latitudes . . . well, seventy degrees or more, then you're approaching a situation where you have permanent darkness during the winter and a permanent brightness – daylight – during the summer.

Caroline Wolf: In the summertime we're in light twenty-four hours a day, and it really does something to you, because you know you've always been taught the sun rises in the east and sets in the west . . . in Barrow that doesn't make sense, because it just circles, and then it starts dipping down in September, and by October 18th it's below the horizon, and we won't see it again.

Ian McCaskill: There is a condition known as Seasonal Affective Disorder, which simply means that some people are really badly affected by a lack of sunlight. This is why in northern parts of Sweden the suicide rate goes through the roof during the dark six winter months. And the cure is very simple; you sit these poor souls in brightly lit rooms, and get them to wear a pair of goggles and shine bright lights at them.

> *Eve of the dawn of the year two thousand;*
> *thousands stand on a far east island;*
> *first to be lit by millennium's morning;*
> *loving the starlight that passes for meaning.*

Caroline Wolf: And some people get real depressed. It's called the dark season.

Song: 'North to Alaska'

Caroline Wolf: Then towards the spring the sun is coming back. In February it starts popping up. The first day ... it's up all of five minutes. But the whole town stops. Everyone just goes out and gazes at the sun.

Ian McCaskill: And this cheers the poor little things up.

Francis Spufford: Once you see that snow you can never quite believe in the fullness of the world any more.

Charles Burton: On 2 September 1979, we set out to do what we called the TransGlobe Expedition, which was to go south to Antarctica, then up the date-line on the other side, then up to the Pole, and south to Greenwich. And that was going to take us ... well, it did take us three years.

Sir Ranulph Fiennes: This particular area here we have got ridge-walls of blue ice blocks between twelve and fifteen feet high. To get through these . . .

Charles Burton: It's always moving the whole time. It can break up while you're on it. Obviously the worst thing about that is if you're in bed, in your tent, and the ice cracks under you, you've actually got no chance.

Francis Spufford: . . . on the other hand, you get someone like Charlotte Brontë. For her, the extreme coldness of the poles was more important, as a metaphor for the state of the human heart . . .

Charles Burton: Coping with yourself . . . the loneliness . . . is basically inbred. The idea is to lock yourself away . . . you can't go out for a walk – you'd get lost and you'd die.

TransGlobe HQ, Telephone Call: Hello, TransGlobe, London. You're calling from Resolute Bay, yes. You have? What is it, please? My team has arrived at the North Pole! Thanks very much. Reception very poor, very poor, but I confirm, I copy . . .

Song: Frank Black – '(I Want to Live on an) Abstract Plain'

Francis Spufford: It was almost a journey into abstraction to go to the North . . . there's so much room to bring to it whatever you want to put in . . .

Charles Burton: The only way you can find out if you're at the North Pole is to take a theodolite reading of the sun at noon, and also for it to be verified by a plane coming over. I mean, Wally Herbert drifted through it while he was asleep . . .

David Broughton: I first flew over the North Pole in 1967, and have been more than twenty-five times since, specifically to test equipment at very high latitudes. We invariably do a few circuits, so that one is circumnavigating the world in just a couple of minutes.

Gloria Clifton: . . . It means that once you get close to the poles a magnetic compass is useless. It's just pointing down into the centre of the Earth . . .

David Broughton: . . . It's embedded in the core of the Earth, and the field is very roughly aligned north and south . . .

Gloria Clifton: . . . and the latest thinking is that when it does happen it will happen pretty quickly, and then we'll be in for a long era of magnetic polarity being at the south . . .

David Broughton: . . . there are many animals that do have an ability to tell north, magnetic north, quite naturally. This is thought to be due to residual magnetite, usually around the eye area in the skull.

Dr Robin Baker: . . . or molecules resonating at the back of the retina . . .

Francis Spufford: . . . and I think our idea of the North is an endless argument between the real . . .

David Broughton: . . . and it's thought that a small number of human beings have a residual ability to do this . . .

Francis Spufford: . . . and the dreamed . . .

Robin Baker: You'd get them to wear magnetic headphones or bar magnets on their head, and see if they could still judge where north was . . .

Patrick Moore: People often ask me how you find the North Star. Well, it's quite easy. First of all, it's always in the north.

David Broughton: In the northern hemisphere one can anchor the sky on Polaris – the entire sky rotates around that star, and that is, I think, something that locates one a little bit . . . makes one feel comfortable.

News Just In

Look North: Fish in some Yorkshire rivers have lost the ability to swim, and are floundering in the strong winter currents as rainwater pours from the moors. Angling officials, involved in restocking the waterways, are having to train the fish to swim before releasing them into the wild.

We see a dozen or so tiddlers in a scummy paddling pool with water being delivered into it at high pressure through a section of plastic gutter-pipe. Some of the fish brace themselves against the tide, holding their own in the face of the current. Like leaves in a drain in a thunderstorm, others spin and tumble around the pool, too weak to put up a fight, or too smart to bother.

Bridgework

Thou by the Indian Ganges' side
Shoudst rubies find: I by the tide
Of Humber would complain. – Marvell, 'To His Coy Mistress'

To Hull, for a screening of the film about the Humber Bridge you
wrote and presented for the BBC's *Building Sights* programme. The
film's only ten minutes long, so there's a supporting presentation to
begin with, also shot on the bridge, but with a difference. The
man who made it was making his way backwards into the record
books by performing an act of 'reverse pedestrianism' across the
entire length of the bridge. He sported a set of wing mirrors
mounted on his shoulders so he didn't stray from the straight and
narrow, and wore a camera on his head, from where his journey
was captured on celluloid. You thought your film was short, but
his only lasts *three* minutes, which according to your calculations
means that he didn't just walk backwards across the Humber but
set a new record for the 1,500 metres while he was at it.

When you decided on the Humber Bridge as the right place to
make a song and dance about, you thought of it as an act of
celebration, in praise of a structure bigger and better than the
Golden Gate but without the San Francisco skyline as a backdrop
and the Pacific Ocean at its feet. But as the lights go down for
tonight's show, it's a commemoration. Elsewhere, in more exotic
locations, longer roadways and higher towers are nearing com-
pletion, connecting the banks of faster, deeper, wider waters, spanning greater distances of the imagination. In those circumstances,
what you've done with the Humber Bridge is memorialized it.

The Humber Bridge

1. 0':10" *Presenter exits steel door on to connecting parapet atop southern towers. Anorak. Hurricane. Vertigo. To camera:*
From up here in the gods, you really get the feeling that you're part of something fundamental – not just one of the modern wonders of the world, but one of those monumental locations on the surface of the planet. It's not just the longest span, it's also the loneliest, surrounded by lowland or sea level on all sides, which exaggerate its proportions, and make it a landmark in every sense of the word . . .

2. 0':50" *Wide-shot, bridge in profile. Caption: Engineers – Freeman Fox and Partners. Voice-over:*
. . . or a water-mark even, set against those pale horizons of water and sky.

3. 1':05" *Close-up, binocular lenses. Mid-shot, toll-plaza and operators in half-light. Bridge illuminated, headlights reflected in Humber. Voice-over:*
Closed-circuit TV, monitors, surveillance, smoked-glass, uniforms, documents being examined, money changing hands . . . there's something a little bit sinister about the control tower and the toll booths, something a little bit Eastern European, reminiscent of a border crossing or a check-point. The barriers and the signals are the sort you might come up against at a frontier between two continents, and those vehicles making the journey at dawn or at dusk look like they're leaving for a new world across the water.

4. 2':30" *Panning shot: underside of bridge to vanishing point, from north shore. Voice-over:*
The Greenwich Meridian actually crosses the Humber, and if it

were a real thing rather than an imaginary line, it would probably look something like this. Underneath, it's a road to nowhere, giving the impression of being never-ending, or having no real destination or point of arrival, like a rainbow.

5. 2':50" *Driving across bridge, camera through sun roof. Diagonal movement of cables against ocean-coloured sky. Fade to aerial shot, iron-coloured water beneath. Voice-over:*

And on top it's much more than a way of getting from A to B – it's an art installation of some type, honouring the ideals of balance and symmetry and poise. Personally, I find it satisfying that the greatest bridge of its type should be here, spanning the mud flats of Humberside, or the East Riding of Yorkshire, as I still think of it.

6. 3':15" *Camera from helicopter, circling northern towers.*

It's also a tug-of-war going on between two shorelines, or a harp that plays when the wind blows through it, or a cat's cradle strung out across a river.

7. 3':45" *Archive footage of construction. Black and white. Voice-over:*

Or spun out, I should say. It's hard to believe, but the main cables are made up of one continuous strand of wire just a few millimetres thick, and during construction, a spinning wheel carried the thread up and over the shoulders of one tower, out across the river to the far side, and back again, thousands of times, like winding a length of wool on to two outstretched arms.

8. 4':11" *Presenter, close-up of face, fading to metalwork and rigging. Voice-over:*

And the best way of understanding a suspension bridge is to think of a washing line, where the towers are the props, the cable is the line itself and the road is the washing, blowing around in the breeze. It's also about suspension of disbelief, because if you thought about it for too long you'd never set foot on it again – it's completely improbable.

9. 4':26" *Static shot along length of walkway. Presenter passes camera heading towards far distance. Voice-over:*
The bridge is so long it has to take into account the curvature of the earth, which is worth bearing in mind when it comes to walking across it, stepping out into the wild blue yonder.

10. 4':50" *Archive footage, crane hoisting section of bridge from river-barge. Extend and fade to presenter exiting backwards, tortoise-style, through metal hatch, and closing it. Voice-over:*
The roadway itself was the last part of the bridge to be built. It's made up of steel boxes dangling down from above and spliced together. The boxes are hollow, making the inside of the bridge a corridor through hundreds of metal rooms or tanks.

11. 5':20" *From black, strip lights flicker on in each section, randomly, illuminating bridge interior. Effect – white dot on telly when turned off, in reverse. Presenter strides out into it. Voice-over:*
Looking through them is an optical illusion, a trick of the light, a time-tunnel, doors disappearing inside each other all the way to infinity. In summer it's like an oven, and like a freezer in winter, and deafening all year round with the thunder of traffic just inches overhead.

12. 6':15" *Hand-held camera, following presenter through mainten-ance shaft into south-east anchorage. Torch-lit. Effect – Howard Carter. Voice-over:*
This is one of the four inner sanctums, the south-east anchorage where all of the wire that makes up one of the main cables is held in position – by old-fashioned nuts and bolts. You have to keep

reminding yourself that this isn't hundreds and thousands of different wires, it's all one, 22,000 miles of it looped over and lashed together. It could be the inside of a grand piano. Everything here is very finely tuned, highly strung – it's hard not to think of a catapult or a crossbow, drawn back, and there's a precarious silence which seems to match the tension and force and pressure of this place.

13. 7':15" *Close-up of wire. Wide shot of anchorage. Voice-over:*
The wires becomes shafts of light through a high window, played on to a distant wall.

14. 7':53" *Final shot of anchorage space from staircase. Effect – world's biggest squash court. Presenter diminished by scale. Voice-over:*
It's cathedral-like in here. Makes you feel like whispering, or lighting a candle, or leaving money in a box.

15. 8':49" *Presenter on pier afoot south-west tower. Mid-shot, zooming out. To camera:*
Most of the water in the North of England runs through here, so I can think of the bridge as something that symbolizes the coming together of all the rivers and streams that stretch back like arteries into the heart of the country. And going inland, the Humber comes out of the Ouse, which comes out of the Aire, which comes out of the Calder, which comes out of the Colne, which springs in the village where I live. Technically, I could sail home from here. And if I'd been away at sea, this bridge would be the perfect gateway to look out for, and come back through.

Sweeping shot of Humber, southern horizon. Captions: white lettering in bottom left, against smoke-blue backdrop. Credits:

Camera
PATRIC DUVAL

Producer
RUTH ROSENTHAL

Director
KIM FLITCROFT

Evening. Long-shot of bridge in silhouette. White lettering and numerals:

BBC MCMXCV

Over the Top into Lancashire

Driving along the A666 you pass Kearsley Town Hall, the Probation Service building used for meetings, conferences and in-house training. Like most organizations at the social-studies end of things, the Service was mad-keen on any idea or concept vaguely connected to human behaviour, particularly when it came in the form of a game or an exercise designed to throw light on the workings of the mind – especially the criminal one. The more contrived, the better. Theories were handed down like broken toys from organizations that no longer had any use for them or had found they didn't work. At Kearsley we played with them, safely, amongst ourselves, before launching them on the mad and the bad and the downright unlucky of Greater Manchester.

Anyone walking in on those sessions might have thought they were stumbling into an audition for *Playschool* presenters, or had found the place where handmade Christmas cards or peg baskets or letter racks were built and tested before being demonstrated on *Blue Peter*, or were witnessing a meeting of transcendental meditationists or yogic flyers. The carpet would be covered in felt-tips, crayons, sticky-back plastic, egg boxes and toilet-roll holders, or the air would be full of balloons and the walls covered with posters. People would be holding hands in circles with their eyes closed, or crawling around on all fours, or falling backwards into each others' arms, or imagining themselves to be farmyard animals or trees, or videoing colleagues pretending to be glue-sniffers or bank robbers or penniless drunks demanding cash.

Somewhere in the middle, a 'coordinator' or 'facilitator' or 'trainer' would be calling the shots and making the next humiliating suggestion, like the ringmaster in a big top. Obligingly, the seals balanced balls on their noses and the elephants stood on their hind legs, begging for buns.

There was something very fishy about the whole business, something mildly Californian and 1970s about it all. The biggest puzzle was how thoughts and practices from a garbage can in a Los Angeles drama-therapy workshop had found their way to a decommissioned local-authority headquarters just outside Bolton twenty years later. But like the professionals we were, we got on with it.

A first experience of Kearsley set the standard for all future visits. In an exercise designed to put us in touch with our body language, we were all invited to select a sealed envelope that contained a word describing a human emotion. Turning to the colleague on our right, we then had to demonstrate that emotion using facial gestures only. The colleague had to identify the emotion, and then it was his or her turn, and so on.

Finding the word LOVE inside your envelope, you turned to the tall shy man who'd taken the seat next to you, and in the spirit of the occasion, beamed lovingly at him, summoning up all those achingly precious moments of devotion and desire, and shutting out the image of the pale, bespectacled and bewildered man only six inches from your lips. Just at the point where you wondered if you might have to actually kiss him, he nodded his head and asked, 'Is it HATE?'

There was a moment of tense silence, before he further misinterpreted an expression of dumbfoundedness for one of agreement, and went on to announce, 'It is HATE, isn't it? I thought so.'

Screwing up your piece of paper and passing him the pile of

envelopes, you said, 'Yes, HATE is exactly what it is,' and the group responded with a brief round of applause.

During the same week, in a session billed as 'Creative Working with Clients', you were introduced to the concept of button-sculpting. Each member of the group was provided with a sheet of A2 paper to be spread on the floor. Then from a bucket of assorted buttons and objects of a similar size, everyone selected items that represented 'significant persons' in their life. The buttons or whatever then had to be placed on the paper at meaningful distances from each other, making a sort of solar system of family and friends.

For you, this couldn't have been easier. You fished out the four necessary tokens from the bucket and put them in their correct positions. Then you sat and watched as other group members embarked on the most complicated undertakings: buttons as far away from each other as geometrically possible, buttons overlapping each other and balanced on their side, buttons underneath the paper, buttons broken in half. Close by, a woman who had delved deep into the bucket organized the siege of a toy soldier with three pearl beads and a brooch, and across the far side of the room a man was attempting something intricate with a pipe-cleaner, a bottle top and two paracetamol introduced from his own pocket. Against all this, your own constellation looked pathetic, normal, boring. The facilitator, one of a breed of people never to miss the opportunity of mistaking a tin of beans for a can of worms, or vice versa, sidled up behind you and looked down at your neat little cluster.

'Who have we got here, then?' she wondered.

I talked her through the grouping. The big silver button with a heraldic design embossed on it, like the button from a battledress: my father. Next to it, a smaller, purple, satin-covered button with criss-cross lilac stitching trimming its border: my mother. Next to that, my sister: a custard-yellow glass marble with two red dimples at its poles and a milky white river flowing around its equator. And next to that, the polished silver sixpence of yourself, heads or tails, making a shining full stop to the descending order of items.

She wandered around the formation, looking at it from all angles, thinking of something to say.

'Interesting', she eventually managed, 'how your family play such a central and orderly role in your life.'

I stared up at her from the floor. 'You think so?'

Not all the training exercises were as innocently banal as button-sculpting. On the first day of a three-day course dealing with sexual abuse, we were told of the difficulties that abuse victims face when attempting to disclose offences committed against them. To demonstrate this 'in an experiential way', we were asked to turn to the nearest person, and were given five minutes to disclose a sexual secret of our own. This would be done 'with the strict confidence of your partner, and within the safe and secure atmosphere of the course'. Sensing a disaster, certain members of the group decided instinctively not to play along, and chatted to each other about the weather. But a friend of yours told you afterwards that he'd sat there looking at the floor for four and a half minutes in heavy silence, then feeling the pressure of participation weighing on him, and noticing every other couple talking away merrily, blurted out to the woman sitting next to him, 'I wank two or three times a day.' The woman – virtually a complete stranger – was so shocked and unable to respond that she stared at him, open-mouthed, until the facilitator clapped his hands and turned to the next sheet on his flip-chart.

On yet another course, we were told to draw a line down the centre of a large piece of paper, and on one side list the things in our lives we liked and wanted to keep, and on the other side list the things we'd like to get rid of.

'It doesn't matter how serious or how simple. If it's what you feel, you write it down.'

The woman next to you, as part of the inventory of things she could well live without, included the entry, 'wobbly bits'. You nudged your friend and pointed with your eyes at what she'd written, and he strolled over and stood behind her to read the paper. What he then said, and the way he said it, was meant as an act of generosity and support towards a like-minded colleague. If she had the courage to write such a thing in front of a group of people she didn't know from Adam, then he for one was going to stand by her, and let her know she was amongst friends.

Unfortunately, his eyesight wasn't what it might have been from that range. Additionally, most employees of the Service at the time spent most of their days in the outer reaches of the right-on-osphere. So putting his arm around her and saying, 'Don't you worry, darling, I like your wobbly bits,' would have been inappropriate enough in itself, but the fact that he'd misread the 'b' of bits for a 't' made it an actionable offence of epic proportions. Fortunately embarrassment intervened, followed by the facilitations of the facilitator, happily inviting us all back to our seats as he explained how we might put such an exercise into use with our clients. 'And don't worry about spelling or anything like that. It's the thought that counts.'

On one of the last courses you ever attended, you were given a piece of flesh-coloured cardboard and a pair of scissors, and asked to cut the card into a shape that represented some event from the past that you could then go on to talk about. Thinking that you'd try and invent a story about a family sailing holiday (we'd never been on a sailing holiday, possibly because your dad was once seasick on the two-hour cruise from Bridlington Harbour to

Scarborough Head and back), you cut the piece into a shape that roughly resembled a mast, then waited your turn. But when the card was pinned on the square of black paper in front of the group, it threw up an altogether different memory – a real one – and before you knew what was happening, you were spilling the beans.

You had your first collision with the world of visual art when you were nine, or maybe ten. Dad was working for the Probation Service somewhere in Lancashire, and one night arrived home declaring he'd become a member of Oldham Picture Lending Library. He'd brought back his first painting which would hang in our house for a month. It was wrapped in a plastic bag, and as he undid it, you saw the library stamp on a piece of yellow paper glued to the back, and the length of frayed string to hang it with. When he flipped it over, it was as if he'd made an announcement that no one knew how to deal with – like we were going to emigrate to Canada on Tuesday, or for the last twenty years he'd been working for MI5. Not that a print of Salvador Dali's *Christ of St John of the Cross* is particularly shocking or blasphemous, but introduced into a medium-size end-terrace on the side of a hill in West Yorkshire, its presence takes a little bit of coming to terms with. Mum studied Dad's beaming face for clues, looked again at the picture, and went into the kitchen. Dad took down a water-colour of one of the local villages and lifted the crucified Christ on to a nail on the wall, mirroring for a moment the outstretched arms of the man on the cross. He stood back to admire it, readjusting it a couple of times to make sure it was straight, then disappeared upstairs to get into his gardening clothes.

Left alone with *Christ of St John of the Cross*, you sat at his feet and stared up at the man with his face buried in his chest, tipped forward, top-heavy, floating above an estuary at low tide and a boat tethered to a post.

Odd. Very odd. What made it stranger was the fact that the settee and armchairs from the front-room had been taken away that week to be reupholstered, and replaced by seats and office furniture borrowed by your father from the Probation Service waiting-room in Ashton. That evening we ate our tea on a metal bench with a green foam cover, watching the telly, our backs to the toppling figure of Christ of St John of the Cross, with only the strong nails driven through both palms keeping him from crashing head-first on to the formica coffee-table in front of the gas fire.

Writing

You come downstairs at about half-seven and start writing, because there's nothing else to do. You don't smoke and you've run out of coffee. The next time you look at the clock it's two in the afternoon. You're hypothermic – shivering in the cold room, dizzy with hunger.

Writing is a form of disappearance. Burglars watching the house from outside for four or five hours would think it empty. There isn't another human activity which combines stillness and silence with so much energy. The mind on red-alert, the body almost closed down. The modern world expects action and noise whenever effort takes place – you've been in situations where people have forgotten you exist, where you've written yourself into invisibility. Writing is time on your own, unavoidable loneliness, a drift away from the apparent and the appreciable into a state of breath, thought, and micro-movements of the hand only. You've read about people who can slow their heartbeat down to almost nothing, who can bring about a sort of controlled coma. You've heard it said that mountain climbers on the summit of Everest are experiencing a slow death at the same time as celebrating their ultimate achievement, because of the lack of oxygen at that altitude.

You mention these things to a friend in a letter. He writes back and tells you why it's harder to write as you get older. Not because of a lack of ideas or enthusiasm, but because it's too much like dying.

News Just In

The *Yorkshire Post*. South Yorkshire police have been criticized after organizing an identity parade that turned into a farce. A black defendant, Mr Martin Kamara, was originally to be placed in a line-up with eight white men, but in an attempt to make the parade more fair, police called in a make-up artist to paint the white men black. Mr Kamara, walking free from court, said, 'It was like an audition for an Al Jolson show. The whole process was just laughable. As the white men stood in the line-up, the heat and the bright lights made their make-up run and smudge. The white men were standing there with their faces blacked up, but their hands were still white.' Mr Kamara, who is six-foot-three and bald headed, describes himself as a Salford-born, half-Irish half-West-African Mancunian. A police spokeswoman said, 'We were faced with the difficult job of finding men similar in appearance to Mr Kamara, and could not find suitable men of the same ethnic origin.' The judge in the case has criticized the police, and the charge against Mr Kamara – one of blackmail – has been dropped.

Lighting-Up Time

I preached near Huddersfield to the wildest congregation I have seen in Yorkshire, yet they were restrained by an unseen hand. John Wesley's Journal, 1759

Christmas Eve, you walk down to the Christingle service in the village with your mother, and Laurie your niece and Jonathan your nephew. Christingle is a junior version of Midnight Mass, introduced to discharge some of the static electricity that most children are primed with at this time of year, and to try to connect Christmas with the Church. Tonight, St Bartholomew's has a full house, side to side and front to back, but apparently it isn't as full as in years gone by, when the kids ran riot and the vicar smiled, holding a painted melon above his head, announcing the birth of Jesus.

There's a brief sermon on the Germanic origins of the service, delivered from behind a lectern in the shape of a soaring eagle, giving the vicar the look of an aerobatics stunt-man lashed above the wings of a single-seater plane. Lots of crying and screaming and looking for lost children under pews and behind curtains. A long queue for the one toilet in the vestry. The church like an aviary, full of strange sounds and exotic noises flitting from one wooden beam to another up under the roof.

The high point is the distribution of the Christingles, in which all the children (and some of the excitable adults) surge forward to collect what looks like a First-World-War hand-grenade – an orange with a candle jammed in its navel, stabbed by four cocktail sticks, each sporting a jelly tot or a sultana. Every orange is finished off with a red ribbon around its equator. The vicar reminds us that we hold in our hands the fruit of the earth and the light of the world, and the four seasons and the bread of heaven, and the death, and the resurrection. After receiving their payload, the children perform an orderly procession along the outside aisles and back up the middle, until gridlock occurs. Then all candles are lit, the next from the last, and the house lights are cut. Each child stands with a face like a mask, lit from below. *Away in a Manger* is sung, and you amaze yourself by remembering most of the words, and flush out a couple of tears from each eye by blinking, and take them into your mouth with the tip of your tongue.

The vicar makes his closing remarks, including some safety tips on the extinguishing of the candles. When the lights go on, most of the jelly tots have disappeared, and three eight-year-olds have set fire to the cocktail sticks and are dangling the red ribbons in the flames. A parent steps in as an arson attack on the Lady Chapel looks possible. Another boy drips molten wax into the hood of his brother's anorak, and a little girl spears herself in the nostril while attempting to eat one of the sweets from the wooden skewer. The church is hazy with blue smoke, as if some ancient ritual or powerful act of magic had taken place, involving sacrifice and fire.

The big doors open on to a cold, clear night. Parents lead their families along the churchyard and through the iron gates at the far end, towards Christmas Day morning. Your mother and the children climb into a car and turn the corner. Half a dozen of you stand in the doorway, not in any rush to go anywhere, see anyone.

Under the stars, someone notices the sky, and points out the constellations with the burning, laser-red tip of a cigarette. Aries, grazing in the path of the planets. Orion the hunter, with one foot in the river, lifting his club and his shield to the great orange eye of Taurus the bull. Pegasus, the winged horse, with the fish of Pisces splashing about under its hooves and Andromeda reaching out for its reins. The flickering silver pulse of Sirius just above the horizon – a filling in the mouth of the great dog Canis, bearing its teeth at Lepus the hare. Ursa Major and Ursa Minor, the great bear and its cousin, tethered to Polaris, plodding eternally like circus animals around the North Star. And Gemini, the twins, falling through space together at arm's length, repelled and obsessed at the same time, pushing each other away and hanging on for grim death. Your stars. Your sign.

The cigarette gets flicked away, upwards into the bare branches of trees lining the graveyard, into the Milky Way. Then you split up, go your separate ways, towards different lives under the same patch of the sky.

He just wanted a decent book to read ...

Not too much to ask, is it? It was in 1935 when Allen Lane, Managing Director of Bodley Head Publishers, stood on a platform at Exeter railway station looking for something good to read on his journey back to London. His choice was limited to popular magazines and poor-quality paperbacks – the same choice faced every day by the vast majority of readers, few of whom could afford hardbacks. Lane's disappointment and subsequent anger at the range of books generally available led him to found a company – and change the world.

'We believed in the existence in this country of a vast reading public for intelligent books at a low price, and staked everything on it'
Sir Allen Lane, 1902–1970, founder of Penguin Books

The quality paperback had arrived – and not just in bookshops. Lane was adamant that his Penguins should appear in chain stores and tobacconists, and should cost no more than a packet of cigarettes.

Reading habits (and cigarette prices) have changed since 1935, but Penguin still believes in publishing the best books for everybody to enjoy. We still believe that good design costs no more than bad design, and we still believe that quality books published passionately and responsibly make the world a better place.

So wherever you see the little bird – whether it's on a piece of prize-winning literary fiction or a celebrity autobiography, political tour de force or historical masterpiece, a serial-killer thriller, reference book, world classic or a piece of pure escapism – you can bet that it represents the very best that the genre has to offer.

Whatever you like to read – trust Penguin.